What Matters?

∞

What Matters?

Economics for a Renewed Commonwealth

Wendell Berry

Foreword by Herman E. Daly

COUNTERPOINT

BERKELEY

"Money vs. Goods" was first published in the *Progressive* in two installments
entitled "Inverting the Economic Order" and "The Cost of Displacement";
"The Love of Farming" was first published in *Farming* and in *Harper's*;
"Faustian Economics" first appeared in *Harper's*. The essays in Part II
are from *Another Turn of the Crank*, *Citizenship Papers*, *Home Economics*,
and *What Are People For?*

Library of Congress Cataloging-in-Publication Data
Berry, Wendell, 1934–
What matters? : economics for a renewed commonwealth /
by Wendell Berry ; foreword by Herman E. Daly.
p. cm.
ISBN 978-1-58243-606-7
1. Community development—United States.
2. Sustainable development—United States.
3. Economics—United States. I. Title.
HN90.C6B483 2010
330.1—dc22   2010005451

Cover design by Silverander Communications
Interior design by David Bullen
Printed in the United States of America

COUNTERPOINT
2117 Fourth Street
Suite D
Berkeley, CA 94710

www.counterpointpress.com

Distributed by Publishers Group West

10   9   8   7   6   5   4   3   2   1

We must make our choice between economy
and liberty, or profusion and servitude.

THOMAS JEFFERSON

Contents

Foreword

Herman E. Daly

As a poet, novelist, essayist, farmer, and thinker on matters agrarian, Wendell Berry needs no introduction. But he is not a professional economist, not a guild member with a PhD union card. Nor does he claim to be such. In a world where knowledge is organized by discipline and professionalized in tight circles, it is often hard to be heard outside the circumference of one's own silo. Therefore I fear that the very people for whom reading these essays would be most beneficial, and through whom they could have the most salutary impact on our ailing world, will simply not read them. I can imagine some of my university colleagues and students in economics departments asking: *Why should I read a book by a noneconomist on "economics for a renewed commonwealth"? There likely won't be a single equation in the book, and use of the archaic word "commonwealth" betrays a probable lack of understanding of the individualistic basis of neoclassical economic theory. Economists don't write poetry or fiction (well, maybe a bit of the latter, but not on purpose), so let not poets or agrarian-environmentalist-localists write about the sophisticated technical science of economics in a globalized industrial growth economy. Leave it to the experts to continue to grow the economy and thereby provide the only possible solution to the problems of poverty, energy, and climate change.* I can hear it now, complete with aggrieved intonation.

My purpose in this foreword is therefore to preemptively reply to this imagined but not unlikely invitation for Wendell to shut up. I want to explain why it is critically important for all citizens, especially professional economists, to read and reflect deeply on the essays in this book. Yet I understand the reluctance of someone with the commitments sketched above to give these essays a fair reading. To do so is to run a serious risk of conversion away from the dominant idolatry of our culture—a liberating conversion to be sure, but damned uncomfortable.

What do we economists have to learn from Wendell Berry? Many things, but here I will mention only two. First is a definitional correction regarding the basic nature of our subject matter—exactly what reality matters most to our economic life and why? Second, what mode of thinking does this reality require of us in order to understand it as well as possible, without seducing us into spurious substitutes for honest ignorance?

The definitional correction goes back to Aristotle and, while somewhat retained by the classical economists, seems to have been dropped from the current neoclassical canon. Aristotle distinguished "*oikonomia*" from "*chrematistics.*" Oikonomia is the science or art of efficiently producing, distributing, and maintaining concrete use values for the household and community over the long run. Chrematistics is the art of maximizing the accumulation by individuals of abstract exchange value in the form of money in the short run. Although our word "economics" is derived from oikonomia, its present meaning is much closer to chrematistics. The word chrematistics is currently relegated to unabridged dictionaries, but the reality to which it refers is everywhere present and is frequently and incorrectly called economics. Wendell Berry is, I believe, urging us to correct our definition of economics by restoring to it the meaning of oikonomia and freeing it from confusion with, and excessive devotion to, chrematistics. In replacing chrematistics by oikonomia we not only refocus on a different reality but also embrace the purposes served within that different reality—community, frugality, efficiency, and long-term stewardship of particular places.

Where today do we find chrematistics masquerading as economics? Certainly in the recent Wall Street fiasco—selling a "bet on a debt

[as] an asset" as Wendell succinctly put it. It is amazing that people who have recently engaged in this disastrous stupidity on such a massive scale still have any credibility at all! Yet belief in "free markets" as the philosopher's stone that alchemically transmutes the dross of chrematistics into the gold of oikonomia remains strong.

Other examples of chrematistics at work include monopoly pricing, tax evasion, subsidies, rent seeking, forced mobility of labor, cheap labor from union busting and illegal immigration, off-shoring, mergers, hostile takeovers, usury, and bullying litigation—not to mention the airlines' successful shifting on to their customers the labor previously done by former travel agents, check-in clerks, and baggage handlers. Externalizing environmental costs—shifting the cost of depletion and pollution from the producer to the general public, the future, and other species—is probably the most common and most disastrous chrematistic maneuver. The unaccounted costs range from irksome noise, to mountaintop removal and filling up of valleys with toxic tailings, to a dead zone in the Gulf of Mexico, to global climate change and species extinction. Confusing oikonomia and chrematistics, misdefining the proper subject matter of economics, has deadly consequences. In the face of all this it is hard to remember that there are still some people doing useful work and creating wealth to really benefit the community. Chrematistics has not entirely displaced oikonomia, but it is trying to. In Wendell's terms the little economy is trying to impose its puny logic on the mysteries and complexities of the Great Economy.

Professional economists should thank Wendell for his sharp reminder about what matters. However, if we are too proud to accept correction from a poet and agrarian, we can claim to have rediscovered Aristotle's forgotten definitions all by ourselves. But then we will still be obliged to apply those definitions to the modern world and be brought face to face with the collective fantasy, idiocy, and horror that Wendell has identified and discussed.

The other thing economists can learn from Wendell Berry, as

much from his example as from explicit discussion, has to do with the proper matching of our mode of thinking to the particular reality we are thinking about, and inevitably shaping. Blaise Pascal spoke of two modes of thinking: the "spirit of geometry" and the "spirit of finesse." Similarly, economist Nicholas Georgescu-Roegen recently distinguished thinking with precisely defined analytic concepts that do not overlap with their other, from thinking with dialectical concepts that do overlap with their other at the boundaries. The best example of an analytic concept is a number. It is only itself and does not overlap with any other number. Land and sea would be dialectical concepts because, although for the most part distinct, they must overlap in tidal marshlands, estuaries, beaches, river deltas, or even the continental shelf, if they are to reflect reality. Each of these border areas in some reasonable sense is both land and sea—a logical contradiction but true to reality. Money is a notoriously dialectical concept, overlapping with nonmonetary assets of varying degrees of liquidity. When economists try to impose an analytical definition on money they end up multiplying categories (M_1, M_2, M_3 ...) or failing to capture the shaded subtleties of the borderlands. Analytical concepts employ mathematics to weed out contradictions where "yes-and-no" answers are not allowed. The virtue demanded by analytic thought is rigor; its defect is its inability to deal with qualitative change and evolution. If we do not allow something to overlap with its other then how could it ever evolve into anything different from what it is? The virtue of dialectical thinking is that it can accommodate qualitative change—what used to be dry land can gradually become sea or vice versa. Its defect is that it has to tolerate at least a range of contradiction. The virtue demanded by dialectical thought is good judgment, or as Pascal preferred, "finesse"—finesse in handling contradiction.

Today analytic thought is very much in vogue, and in economics quite dominant. It has the aura of science. Analytic thinking requires a reality that is like a number, and since chrematistics is about the maximization of exchange value numerically measured by money, it tends to attract those with a strong prior commitment to analytical thinking. Dialectical thinking is required by a reality that changes qualitatively through overlapping categories. Oikonomia deals with use values that are embodied in products that evolve over the long run to serve changing wants, and with changing technical efficiency in an evolving community that coheres around values that also change. A preference for dialectical thinking leads to a focus on oikonomia, and vice versa.

My point is not to say that one mode of thought is good and the other bad. Both are clearly necessary. There is a limit to what we can do with numbers, just as there is a limit to what we can do without them. But I do suggest that there is currently a bias toward the analytical and a corresponding prejudice against the dialectical. This quantitative bias is certainly not the only reason for the excessive importance given to chrematistics over oikonomia—greed, avarice, and intellectual sloth play a bigger role-—but I think it is a contributing factor. In sum, the second thing that economists can learn from Wendell Berry's essays is that clear-headed reasoning with dialectical concepts about what matters is possible, necessary, and enlightening. Here Wendell persuades by example.

When a problem yields neither to the spirit of geometry nor to the spirit of finesse, Wendell advises us to be more at home with ignorance and mystery. They are much better companions than either phony equations or empty verbiage, and more congenial to a creature trying to understand the overall workings of Creation and intuit the will of the Creator whose broken image he still bears.

In my eagerness to convince my fellow economists to read this book, I am afraid that I have failed to specifically address the general reader. So, dear general reader, for whom Wendell Berry wrote these essays, let me assure you that if you have read this far, you have gotten through the most obscure and convoluted part of the book. The rest is smooth sailing with a clear-headed and trustworthy navigator, albeit through deep waters. The essays require wakeful attention and focused thought, but priestly intermediation by professional experts is surely not needed.

I

Money Versus Goods

My economic point of view is from ground-level. It is a point of view sometimes described as "agrarian." That means that in ordering the economy of a household or community or nation, I would put nature first, the economies of land use second, the manufacturing economy third, and the consumer economy fourth. The basis of such an economy would be broad, the successive layers narrowing in the order of their diminishing importance.

The first law of such an economy would be what the agriculturalist Sir Albert Howard called "the law of return." This law requires that what is taken from nature must be given back: The fertility cycle must be maintained in continuous rotation. The primary value in this economy would be the capacity of the natural and cultural systems to renew themselves. An authentic economy would be based upon renewable resources: land, water, ecological health. These resources, if they are to stay renewable in human use, will depend upon resources of culture that also must be kept renewable: accurate local memory, truthful accounting, continuous maintenance, un-wastefulness, and a democratic distribution of now-rare practical arts and skills. The economic virtues thus would be honesty, thrift, care, good work, generosity, and (since this is a creaturely and human, not a mechanical, economy) imagination, from which we have compassion. That primary value and these virtues are essential to what we have been calling "sustainability."

A properly ordered economy, putting nature first and consumption last, would start with the subsistence or household economy and proceed from that to the economy of markets. It would be the means by which people provide to themselves and to others the things necessary to support life: goods coming from nature and human work. It would distinguish between needs and mere wants, and it would grant a firm precedence to needs.

A proper economy, moreover, would designate certain things as priceless. This would not be, as now, the "pricelessness" of things that are extremely rare or expensive, but would refer to things of absolute value, beyond and above any price that could be set upon them by any market. The things of absolute value would be fertile land, clean water and air, ecological health, and the capacity of nature to renew herself in the economic landscapes. Our nearest cultural precedent for this assignment of absolute value is biblical, as in Psalm 24 ("The earth is the Lord's, and the fulness thereof . . .") and Leviticus 25:23 ("The land shall be sold forever . . ."). But there are precedents in all societies and traditions that have understood the land or the world as sacred—or, speaking practically, as possessing a suprahuman value. The rule of pricelessness clearly imposes certain limits upon the idea of land ownership. Owners would enjoy certain customary privileges, necessarily, as the land would be entrusted to their intelligence and responsibility. But they would be expected to use the land as its servants and on behalf of all the living.

. . .

The present and now-failing economy is just about exactly opposite to the economy I have just described. Over a long time, and by means of a set of handy prevarications, our economy has become an anti-economy, a financial system without a sound economic basis and without economic virtues.

It has inverted the economic order that puts nature first. This economy is based upon consumption, which ultimately serves, not the ordinary consumers, but a tiny class of excessively wealthy people for whose further enrichment the economy is understood (by them) to exist. For the purpose of their further enrichment, these plutocrats and the great corporations that serve them have controlled the economy by the purchase of political power. The purchased governments do not act in the interest of the governed and their country; they act instead as agents for the corporations.

That this economy is, or was, consumption-based is revealed by the remedies now being proposed for its failure: stimulate, spend, create jobs. What is to be stimulated is spending. The government injects into the failing economy money to be spent, or to be loaned to be spent. If people have money to spend and are eager to spend it, demand for products will increase, creating jobs; industry will meet the demand with more products, which will be bought, thus increasing the amount of money in circulation; the greater amount of money in circulation will increase demand, which will increase spending, which will increase production—and so on until the old fantastical economy of limitless economic growth will have "recovered."

But spending is not an economic virtue. Miserliness is not an economic virtue either. Saving is. Not-wasting is. To encourage spending with no regard at all to what is being purchased may be pro-finance, but it is anti-economic. Finance, as opposed to economy, is always ready and eager to confuse wants with needs. From a financial point of view, it is good, even patriotic, to buy a new car whether you need one or not. From an economic point of view, however, it is wrong to buy anything you do not need. It is unpatriotic too: If you love your country, you don't want to burden or waste it by frivolous wants. Only in a financial system, an anti-economy, can it seem to make sense to talk about "what the economy needs." In an authentic economy, we would ask what the land and the people need. People do need jobs, obviously. But they need jobs that serve natural and human communities, not arbitrarily "created" jobs that serve only the economy.

From an economic point of view, a society in which every school-child "needs" a computer, and every sixteen-year-old "needs" an automobile, and every eighteen-year-old "needs" to go to college is already delusional and is well on its way to being broke.

In a so-called economy that is dependent on indiscriminate spending, "job creation" often implies an ability to "create" new "needs." Until lately this economy has been able to create jobs by creating needs. But this has involved much confusion and a kind of fraud, because it gives no priority to the meeting of needs, and cannot distinguish needs from wants. Our economy, having confused necessities with products or commodities that are merely marketable, deliberately reduces the indispensable service of providing needed goods to "selling" or "marketing" products, some of which have never been and will never be needed by anybody. The gullibility of the public thus becomes an economic resource.

The category of things sold that are not needed now includes even legally marketed foods and drugs. This involves the art (taught and learned in universities) of lying about products. A friend of mine remembers a teacher who said that advertising is "the manufacture of discontent." And so we have come to live in a world in which every brand of painkiller is better than every other brand, in which we have a "service economy" that does not serve and an "information economy" that does not distinguish good from bad or true from false.

The manufacturing sector of a financial system, which does not or cannot distinguish between needs and induced wants, will come willy-nilly into the service of wants, not needs. So it has happened with us. If in some state of emergency our manufacturers were suddenly called upon to supply us with certain necessities—shoes, for example—we would be out of luck. "Outsourcing" the manufacture of frivolities is at least partly frivolous; outsourcing the manufacture of necessities is entirely foolish.

As for the land economies, the academic and political economists seem mainly to ignore them. For years, as I have read articles on the economy, I have waited in vain for the author to "factor in" farming or ranching or forestry. The expert assumption appears to be that the products of the soil are not included in the economy until after they have been taken at the lowest possible cost from those who did the actual work of production, at which time they enter the economy as raw materials for the food, fiber, timber, and lately the fuel industries. The result is inevitable: The industrial system is disconnected from, is unconcerned about, and takes no responsibility for, its natural and human sources. The further result is that these sources are not maintained but merely used and thus are made as exhaustible as the fossil fuels.

As for nature herself, virtually nobody—not the "environmentalist," let alone the economist—regards nature as an economic resource. Nature, especially where she has troubled herself to be scenic, is understood to have a recreational and perhaps an aesthetic value that is to some extent economic. But for her accommodation of our needs to eat, drink, breathe, and be clothed and sheltered, our industrial and financial systems grant her no recognition, honor, or care.

Far from assigning an absolute value to those things we absolutely need, the financial system puts a price, though a highly variable price, on everything. We know from much experience that everything that is priced will sooner or later be sold. And from the accumulating statistics of soil loss, land loss, deforestation, overuse of water, various sorts of pollution, etc., we have reason to fear that everything that is sold will be ruined. When everything has a price, and the price is made endlessly variable by an economy without a stable relation to necessity or to real goods, then everything is disconnected from history, knowledge, respect, and affection—from anything at all that might preserve it—and so is implicitly eligible to be ruined.

What we have been pleased to call our economy does not acknowledge and apparently does not even recognize its continuing absolute dependence on the natural world, on the land economies, and on the work of farmers, ranchers, and foresters—all of which, given the use of available knowledge and precautions, would be self-renewing. At the same time, with a remarkable lack of foresight or even the sight to see what is presently obvious, this economy has made itself absolutely dependent on resources that are either exhaustible by nature or have been made exhaustible by our wastefulness and our refusal to husband and reuse: fossil fuels, metals, and other mined materials. By standards that are utterly absurd, it has long been "too expensive" to salvage perfectly good and usable materials from old buildings, which we knock down or blow up and haul to landfills, and so make even bricks and stones valueless and irrecoverable. Because of falsely cheap materials and energy, we have a "bubble" of houses too big to be heated efficiently or cheaply, or even to be paid for.

To use our agricultural land for the production of "biofuel," as some are now doing, is immediately to raise the question whether it can ever be right to replace food production by the production of a fuel to be burned. If this fuel is produced, like most of our food at present, without the close and loving care that the land requires, then the land becomes an exhaustible resource. Biofuel may be a product of the land and our world-changing technology, but it is just as much a product of ignorance and moral carelessness.

As commodities, the fossil fuels are in a category strictly their own. Unlike other minerals that (in a sensible economy) can be reused, and unlike waterpower that uses water and releases it to be used again, the fossil fuels can be made useful only by being destroyed. They are useful and therefore valuable only in the instant in which they are burning.

To be available for their brief usefulness, these fuels must be dug or pumped from the ground. Their extraction has nearly always damaged, often irreparably, the places and the human communities from which they are taken. For coal to feed the fires by which we live, whole landscapes are destroyed, forests and their soils and creatures are obliterated, streams are covered over, watersheds are degraded and polluted, poisonous residues are left behind, communities are degraded or flooded by toxic wastes or runoff from denuded watersheds, the people are exploited and endangered, their houses damaged, their drinking water poisoned, their complaints and needs ignored. When the fossil fuels, extracted at such a cost to people and nature, are burned, they pollute the atmosphere of all the world, with consequences that are fearful, infamous, and continuing.

In a consciously responsible economy, such abuses would be inconceivable. They could not happen. To damage or destroy an otherwise permanent resource for the sake of a temporary advantage would be readily perceived as senseless by every practical measure and, by the measure of human wholeness, as insane. To value human wants above all the natural and human resources that supply human needs, as the now-failing economy has done, is to run risks and defy paradoxes by which it was and is bound to fail. If we pursue limitless "growth" now, we impose ever-narrower limits on the future. If we put spending first, we put solvency last. If we put wants first, we put needs last. If we put consumption first, we put health last. If we put money first, we put food last. If for some spurious reason such as "economic growth" or "economic recovery," we put people and their comfort first, before nature and the land-based economies, then nature sooner or later will put people last.

But the fossil fuels, which involve destruction for the sake of production and again destruction as a consequence of production, are not the only typical products of our anti-economy. Also typical are products that replace, at high cost, goods that once were cheap or free. The genius of marketing and selling has given us, for example, bottled tapwater, for which we pay more than we pay for gasoline, because of our perfectly rational fear that our unbottled tapwater is polluted. The system of industry, finance, and "marketing" thus makes capital of its own viciousness and of the ignorance and gullibility of a supposedly educated public. By the influence of marketers and sellers, citizens and members are transformed into suckers. And so we have an alleged economy that is not only fire-dependent and consumption-dependent but also sucker-dependent.

For another example, consider the money-drenched entertainment industry. The human species, which has apparently outlived the name Homo sapiens, is said to be something like 200,000 years old. Except for the last seventy-five or so years of their life so far, and except for their decadent ruling classes, most humans have entertained themselves by remembering and telling stories, singing, dancing, playing games, and even by their work of providing themselves with necessities and things of beauty, which usually were the same things. All of this entertainment came free of charge, as a sort of overflow of human nature, local culture, and daily life. Even the beauty of good work and well-made things was a value added at no charge. The entertainment industry has improved upon this great freedom by providing at a high cost, in money but also in health and sanity, an egregiously overpaid corps of entertainers and athletes who tell or perform stories, sing, dance, and play games for us or sell games to us as we passively consume their often degrading productions. The wrong here may be at root only that of an inane and expensive redundancy. If you can read and have more imagination than a doorknob, what need do you have for a "movie version" of a novel?

· · ·

This strange economy produces, typically and in the ordinary course of business, products that are destructive or fraudulent or unnecessary or useless, or all four at once. Another of its typical enterprises is remarkable for the production of what I suppose we will have to call no-product, or no product but money (to the extent that this works). The best-known or longest infamous example of a no-product financial industry is the practice of usury, which is to say the lending of money at exorbitant interest or (some have said) at any interest. In our cultural tradition, as opposed to financial precedent, the condemnation of usury seems to be unanimous.

The Hebrew Bible speaks emphatically against usury in ten of its chapters (by my count), calling it by name, but without much explanation, assuming apparently that its wrongfulness is obvious. From the context it is clear that usury is understood as an injustice and an offense against charity. It is a way for people of wealth to exploit the poor, whom they have been instructed to care for. Only the wealthy have a surplus of money to lend, and they should not use it to take advantage of the needs of others. Usury, moreover, cannot be consistent with the command (Leviticus 19:18) that "thou shalt love thy neighbor as thyself."

Aristotle in *The Nicomachean Ethics* also condemns usury and in language that is remarkably consistent with my description of our own economic malpractice. He classes usurers with pimps, as people who take "anything from any source" or who "take more than they ought and from wrong sources" (the Oxford edition, translated by Sir David Ross).

Dante is perfectly consistent with the Bible and Aristotle when he places the usurers in Hell (*Inferno* XI) with others who are guilty of violence against God. Virgil, explaining this fault to Dante, makes the case clearly and usefully. Usury is a violence against God because it is a violence against nature. Nature is the art of God, just as productive work, the making of useful things, is the art of humans. Humans prosper rightly when their goods come from nature by their good work. Usurers prosper, on the contrary, by making money grow from itself (by "making their money work for them," as we say), thus holding in contempt both nature and work, both divine art and human art.

Ezra Pound, a poet of our own time, was in Dante's tradition when he wrote the two versions of his eloquent poem against usury (*Cantos XLV* and LI). Pound who was (I hope) insane when at his worst, was perfectly sane when he wrote this:

> *With usury has no man a good house*
> *made of stone, no paradise on his church wall*
> *With usury the stone cutter is kept from his stone*
> *the weaver is kept from his loom by usura*
> *Wool does not come into market*
> *the peasant does not eat his own grain*
> *the girl's needle goes blunt in her hand*
> *The looms are hushed one after another*
> . . . .
>
> *Usury kills the child in the womb*
> *And breaks short the young man's courting*
> *Usury brings age into youth; it lies between the bride*
> *and the bridegroom*
> *Usury is against Nature's increase.*

The point—as I understand it, though I understand also that this poem offers far more than a point—is that when money is misused to grow from itself into heaps in the possession inevitably of fewer and fewer people, it cannot be rightly used for the production of goods or even to maintain the subsistence of the people. Workers will not be well paid for good work. The arts will not flourish, and neither will nature.

I need to say here that this issue of usury is far from simple, and that I am not capable even of giving usury a proper definition. The issue is simple only if usury is defined as the taking of *any* interest. It is so defined by Jesus in the Gospel of Luke (6:34–35):

> And if ye lend to them of whom ye hope to receive, what thank have ye? for sinners also lend to sinners, to receive as much again.
>
> But love ye your enemies, and do good, and lend, hoping for nothing again . . .

Such free lending would be possible among neighbors or in a small local economy, but in general we appear to be far from that, the churches along with the rest. In an extensive economy using money, banks appear to be necessary. If the poor, for instance, are to rise above their poverty, or if the young are to acquire houses or farms or small businesses, there probably needs to be an established means of lending them money, and that would be banking. If we are to have banks and banking, then we have to build and equip and maintain the necessary buildings, return a fair dividend to the necessary investors, and pay fair wages or salaries to the necessary employees. The needed funds would have to come to a considerable extent from interest on loans. If the money were to be loaned at no charge, there soon would be no lending institution and nobody to make loans.

And so we come to the uneasy question of what rate of interest would be neither too little nor too much. If too little, loans cannot be made. If too much, then lending becomes, not a service, but the exploitation and even the ruin of borrowers. I don't think a fair rate can be determined according to standards that are only financial. It would have to be determined by responsible bankers, acting also as community members, in the context of their community, local nature, and the local economy.

Such a determination, I believe, can take place only in a bank that is locally owned, conforming in scale to the size and needs of the local community, and by bankers who are aware that the prosperity of the bank is not and can never be separated from the prosperity of the community.

I know from my own experience and observation that a bank of community scale, owned principally by local investors, understanding its dependence on responsible service first of all to local customers—even in a fevered and delirious economy—can function usefully and considerately as a part of the community. Such a bank does not, because if it is to survive it cannot, adopt the lending practices that resulted in our recent housing bubble. In such a bank the loan officers understand necessarily that their responsibility is to the borrowers as much as to the bank. In a locally owned community bank, the lender is a neighbor of the borrower. You don't put your neighbors into trouble or into ruin by misleading them to assume debts they cannot pay—which ultimately, of course, would ruin the lender.

It is clear that if interest rates are not limited by a reasonable, workable concept of fairness, enforceable by law, then they will become exorbitant. Moreover, they are apt to become highly variable according to the whim of lenders inclined to "take more than they ought."

Among its other wrongs, usury destabilizes the relation of money to goods. So does inflation. So does the speculative trading in mortgages, "futures," and "commercial paper" that gives a monetary value to commodities having no present existence or no existence at all. To inflate or obscure the value of money in relation to goods is in effect to steal both from those who spend and from those who save. It is to subordinate real value to a value that is false.

By destabilizing the relation of money to goods, a financial system usurps an economy. Then, instead of the exchange of money for goods or goods for money, we have the conversion of goods into money, in the process often destroying the goods. Money, instead of a token signifying the value of goods, becomes a good in itself, which the wealthy can easily manipulate in their own favor. This is sometimes justified (by the favored) as freedom, as in "free trade" or "the free market," but such a freedom is calculated to reduce substantially the number of the free. The tendency of this freedom necessarily is toward monopoly—toward the one economic entity that will own or control everything. The undisguised aim of Monsanto, for example, is to control absolutely the economy of food. It would do so by setting its own price on its products sold to dependent purchasers who can set a price neither on what they buy nor on what they sell.

To permit so much wealth, power, influence, and ambition to one corporation is an egregious error in a polity supposedly democratic. From the point of view of nature and agriculture, it is an error even larger and more dangerous. For by this error agriculture is forced to subserve the rule of industrialism, which is in most respects antithetical to the healthful practice of agriculture and to the laws of nature, by which, and only by which, agriculture can be made sustainable.

The dominance of agriculture by agribusiness is made possible by the dominance of the economy by interests that are industrial or purely financial. Agribusiness is immensely more profitable monetarily than agriculture, which customarily for the last fifty or sixty years has been either barely profitable or unprofitable. Hence the drastic decline in the agricultural population. One cost of this error is economic injustice, characteristic of industrialism, to the people who do the work: ranchers, farmers, and farm workers. Another cost is first agricultural and then ecological: Under the rule of industrialism the land is forced to produce but is not maintained; the fertility cycle is broken; soil nutrients become water pollutants; toxic chemicals and fossil energy replace human work.

We have allowed, and even justified as "progress," a fundamental disconnection between money and food. And so we are led to the assumption, by ignorant leaders who apparently believe it, that if we have money we will have food, an assumption that is destructive of agriculture and food. It is a superstition just as wicked, and hardly different from, the notion that the world is conformable to our wants and we can be whatever we want to be.

Apparently it takes a lot of money, a lot of power, and even a lot of education to obscure the knowledge that food comes from the land and from the human ability to cause the land to produce and to remain productive. Under the rule of an economy perverted by industrial and financial presumptions, we are destroying both the land and the human means of using the land and caring for it.

We are destroying the land by exposing it to erosion, by infusing it year after year with toxic chemicals (which incidentally poison the water), by surface mining, and by so-called development. We are destroying the cultures and the communities of land use and land husbandry by deliberately slanting the economy of the food system against the primary producers.

We are losing and degrading our agricultural soils because we no longer have enough competent people available to take proper care of them. And we will not produce capable and stewardly farmers, ranchers, and foresters by what we are calling "job creation." The fate of the land is finally not separable from the fate of the people of the land (and the fate of country people is finally not different from the fate of city people). Industrial technology does not and cannot adequately replace human affection and care. Industrial and financial procedures cannot replace stable rural communities and their cultures of husbandry. One farmer, if that name applies, cannot farm thousands of acres of corn and soybeans in the Midwest without production costs that include erosion and toxicity, which is to say damages that are either long-term or permanent.

The farm population has now declined almost to nonexistence because, since the middle of the last century, we have deliberately depressed farm income while allowing production costs to rise, for the sake of "cheap food" and to favor agribusiness. No wonder that farm-raised young people have been moving into the cities and suburbs by millions for two generations, leaving the farms without heirs or successors. The young people decide against too much investment and too much work for too little return. Even if they love farming or ranching enough to want to stay, paying the inevitable economic and personal penalties, they are more than likely to find that they cannot buy land and pay for it by using it. The one reason for this is the disequilibrium between the economy of money and the land economies. Professional people in the cities, who have done well financially, have been "investing" in farmland and rangeland and so lifting the market value of the land above the reach of farmers and ranchers who are *not* doing well economically. The result is that we have an enormous population of dependent people with the subservient mentality of industrial employees, helpless to feed themselves, who are being fed by the tiniest minority of exploited people and from land that is more cruelly exploited than the people.

If we are destroying both the productive land and the rural communities and cultures, how can we assume that money will somehow attract food to us whenever we need it? If, on the contrary, we should decide to right the economic balance by paying a just price to producers, then money could revert to its proper function of encouraging and supporting both food production and the proper husbanding of the land. This, if it could happen, would solve a number of problems. The right answer to urban sprawl, for example, is to make agriculture pay well enough that farmers and ranchers would want to keep the land in use, and their children would want to inherit it to use.

To a ground-level observer, it is obvious that the economic failures I have described involve moral issues of the gravest sort. An essentially immoral system of economy-as-finance, or an economy run by the sole standard of monetary profit, has been allowed to flourish to the point of catastrophe by a fairly general consent to the proposition that economy and morality are two professional specialties that either do not converge, or that can be made to converge by a simple moral manipulation, as follows.

In 1986 the "conservative" columnist William Safire wrote that "Greed is finally being recognized as a virtue . . . the best engine of betterment known to man." This was not, I think, the news that Mr. Safire thought it was, but was merely a repetition of a time-worn rationalization. What may have been new was the "professional" falsehood that greed is the exclusive motive in every choice—that, for example, the *only* way to have good teachers or good doctors is to pay them a lot of money.

Mr. Safire's error, and that of the people he spoke for, is in the idea that everybody can be greedy up to some limit—that, once you have made greed a virtue, it will not crowd out other virtues such as temperance or justice or charity. The virtuously greedy perhaps would agree to let one another be greedy, so long as one person's greed did not interfere with the greed of another person. This would be the Golden Rule of greedy persons, who no doubt would thank God for it.

But that rule appears to be honored entirely in the breach. There are still a good many people who choose or accept a vocation that will not make them rich—many teachers, for instance, and most writers. But for the greedy there appears to be no such concept as *greedy enough*. The greedy consume the poor, the moderately prosperous, and each other with the same relish and with an ever-growing appetite.

Part two of Mr. Safire's error is his assumption that we can restrict the honor of virtuehood to greed alone, leaving the other sins to pine away in customary disfavor: "I hold no brief," he said, "for Anger, Envy, Lust, Gluttony, Pride . . . or Sloth." But he was already too late. A glance at magazine advertising in 1986 would have suggested that these sins had been virtues of commerce long enough already to be taken for granted. As we have sometimes been told, the sins, like the virtues, are inclined to enjoy one another's company.

Mr. Safire's announcement was not a moral innovation, but rather a confession of the depravity of what in 1986 we were calling, and are still calling, "the economy"—a ramshackle, propped-up, greed-enforced anti-economy that is delusional, vicious, wasteful, destructive, hard-hearted, and so fundamentally dishonest as to have resorted finally to "trading" in various pure-nothings. Might it not have been better and safer to have assumed that there is no partition between economy and morality, that the test of both is practicality, and that morality is long-term practicality?

The problem with "the economy" is not only that it is anti-economic, destructive of the natural and human bases of any authentic economy, but that it has been out of control for a long time. At the root of our problem, we now need to suppose, is industrialism and the Industrial Revolution itself. As the original Luddites saw clearly and rightly, the purpose of industrialism from the first has been to replace human workers with machines. This has been justified and made unquestionable by the axiom that machines, according to standards strictly mechanical, work more efficiently and cheaply than people. They answer directly the perpetual need of the greedy to get more for less. This is yet another of our limitless "progressive" ideas: The industrial academics or academic industrialists who subserve the technological cutting edge are now nominating robots as substitutes for parents, nurses, and surgeons. Soon, surely, we will have robots that can worship and make love faster and cheaper than we mere humans, who have been encumbered in those activities by flesh and blood and our old-fashioned ways.

But to replace people by machines is to raise a difficult, and I would say an urgent, question: What are the replaced people to do? Or, since this is a question not all replaced people have been able to answer satisfactorily for themselves, What is to be done with or for them? This question has never received an honest answer from either liberals or conservatives, communists or capitalists. Replaced people have entered into a condition officially euphemized as "mobility." If you have left your farm or your country town and found a well-paying city job or entered a profession, then you are said to have been "upwardly mobile." If you have left the country for the city with visions of bright lights and more money, or if you have gone to the city because you have been replaced as a farm worker by machines and you have no other place to go and you end up homeless or living in a slum without a job, then I suppose you are downwardly mobile—but this is still "progress," for at least you have been relieved of "the idiocy of rural life" or the "mind-numbing work" of agriculture.

When replacement leads to "mobility" or displacement, and displacement leads to joblessness or homelessness, then we have a problem as characteristic of the industrialized world as land waste and pollution. To this problem the two political sides have produced nonsolutions that are hopeless and more cynical (I hope) than many of their advocates realize: versions of "Get a job," job training, job retraining, "better" education, job creation, and "safety nets" such as welfare, Social Security, varieties of insurance, retirement funds, etc. All of these "solutions," along with joblessness itself, serve the purposes of an economy of bubbling money. And every one of them fails to address the problem of "mobility," which is to say a whole society that is socially and economically unstable. In this state of perpetual mobility, even the most lucratively employed are likely to be homeless, if "home" means anything at all, for they are endlessly moving at the dictates of their careers or at the whims of their employers.

To escape the cynicism, heartlessness, and damage implicit in all this mobility, it is necessary to ask another question: Might it not have been that these replaced and displaced people were needed in the places from which they were displaced? I don't mean to suggest that this is a question easily answered, or that anybody should be required to stay put. I do mean that the question ought to be asked. It ought to be asked if only because it calls up another question that might lead to actual thinking: By what standard, or from what point of view, are we permitted to suppose that the displaced people were not needed in their original places? According to the industrial standard and point of view, persons are needed only when they perform a service valuable to an employer. When a machine can perform the same service, a person then is not needed.

Not-needed persons must graduate into mobility, which will take them elsewhere to a job newly vacated or "created," or to job training, or to some safety net, or to netlessness, joblessness, and homelessness. But this version of "not-needed" fits uncomfortably into the cultural pattern by which we define ourselves as civilized or humane or human. It grates achingly against the political and religious traditions that have affirmed for us the inherent worth and even preciousness of individual people. Our mobility, whether enforced or fashionable, has dismembered and scattered families and communities. Politicians and opinion dealers from far left to far right predictably and loudly regret these disintegrations, prescribing for them (in addition to the "solutions" already mentioned) year-round schools, day care, expert counseling, drugs, and prisons.

And so: Might it not be that the displaced persons were needed by their families and their neighbors, not only for their economic assistance to the home place and household, but for their love and understanding, for their help and comfort in times of trouble? Of the Americans known to me, only the Amish have dealt with such questions openly and conscientiously as families, neighbors, and communities. The Amish are Amish by choice. There is no requirement either to subscribe to the religion or to stay in the community. The Amish have their losses and their failures, as one would expect. Lately some of their communities have become involved in the failure of the larger economy. But their families and communities nevertheless have been held together by principle and by the deliberate rejection of economic and technological innovations that threaten them. With the Amish—as once with the rest of us—a family member or a neighbor is by definition needed, and is needed not according to any standard of usefulness or any ratio of cost and price, but according to the absolute standards of kindness, mutuality, and affection. Unlike the rest of us, the Amish have remembered that the best, most dependable, most kind safety net or social security or insurance is a coherent, neighborly, economically sound, local community.

To speak of the need for affection and loyalty and social stability is not at all to slight the need for life-supporting work. Of course people need to work. Everybody does. And in a money-using economy, people need to earn money by their work. Even so, to speak of "a job" as if it were the only economic need a person has, as if it doesn't matter what the job is or where a person must go in order to have it, is brutally reductive. To speak so is to leave out virtually everything that is humanly important: family and community ties, connection to a home place, the questions of vocation and good work. If you have "a job," presumably, you won't mind being a stranger among strangers in a strange place, doing work that is demeaning or unethical or work for which you are unsuited by talent or calling.

When people accept mobility as a condition of work, it means that they have accepted a kind of homelessness. It used to be a part of good manners to ask a person you had just met, "Where are you from?" That question has now become a social embarrassment, for it is too likely to be answered, "I'm not from anywhere." But to be not from anywhere is part of the definition of helplessness. Mobility is a condition in which you can do little or nothing to help yourself, and in which you live apart from family and old neighbors who would be the people most likely to help you.

Usury, for example, is "a job." But it happens to be a job that nobody ought to do. It is a violence against fellow humans who happen to be in need, a violence against work, or against good work, a violence against nature, and therefore (for those to whom it matters) a violence against God. It is a job also that estranges and isolates one from other people, who are perceived by the usurer, not as neighbors, but as potential victims.

To be mobile is not only to be in a new sense homeless. It is also to be in an old sense landless. If you have plenty of money to buy the necessities of life, and the stores are well-stocked with those necessities, then you may not see landlessness as a threat. But suppose you are a poor migrant, black or white, from the cotton or cane fields of the South or the Appalachian coal fields, and you wind up jobless in some "inner city." You have come from the country, and now, cooped up in a strange and unyielding place, without the mutual usefulness of a functioning neighborhood, you experience a helplessness that is new to you: the practical difficulty or impossibility of helping or being helped by somebody you know. A most significant part of that helplessness is the impossibility of helping yourself, and this is the condition of landlessness. I am not talking here about owning land, but merely of having access to it or the use of it. In your new circumstances of displacement, you have no place to grow a garden or keep a few chickens or gather firewood or hunt or fish. Maybe you were, by the official definition, poor where you came from, but there your abilities to do for yourself and others were given scope and efficacy by the landscape. You have come, in short, to the difference, defined by Paul Goodman a long time ago, between competent poverty and abject poverty. A home landscape enables personal subsistence but also generosity. It enables a community to exist and function.

When country people leave home to find work, even when "jobs" are available, they incur liabilities that cannot easily be discounted. The liabilities of homelessness and landlessness may not be noticeable in times of easy money and lots of stuff to buy. But in a time of economic failure and rising unemployment, as now, the liabilities once again rise undeniably into view.

Now the following sentences by Lowell H. Harrison and James C. Klotter, in *A New History of Kentucky*, make a different sense than they would have made to most readers a year ago:

> Yet [in the 1930s] the commonwealth weathered the drought and the floods and survived the depression better than many places. . . . [The] general absence of industry meant relatively little damage there, the overall lack of wealth left people only a little way to fall, and the rural nature of the commonwealth allowed families to live off the land. In fact, people returned to Kentucky, and the decade of the 1930s saw the state's population increase faster than the national average. . . . From distant places, those who had migrated in search of jobs that were now gone came home to crowd in with their families . . .

They "came home" because at home they still had families who were growing a garden, keeping a milk cow, raising chickens, fattening hogs, and gathering their cooking and heating fuel from the woods. Now, eighty years and much "progress" later, where will the jobless go? Not home, for there are no 1930s homes to go to.

Since the end of the Great Depression, and even more since the end of World War II, country people have crowded into the cities. They have come because they have attended colleges and been "overeducated" for country life. They have come for available jobs. They have come because television and the movies have taught them to be unhappy in their "provincial" or "backward" or "nowhere" circumstances. They have come because machines have displaced them from their work and their homes. Many who have come were already poor, and were entirely unprepared for a life away from home. Immense numbers of them have ended up in slums. Some live from some variety of "safety net." Some, the homeless or insane or addicted poor, sleep in doorways or under bridges. Some beg or steal.

In the long run, these surplus people, the not-needed, have overfilled the "labor pool" and so have made labor relatively cheap. If we run short of exploitable poor people in the United States, then we "outsource" our work to the exploitable poor of other countries. Industrial workers and labor unions are having a hard time, and so are farmers, ranchers, and farm workers. People who do the actual work of producing actual products must expect to work cheap, for they are not of the quality of the professionals who "deserve" to charge too much for their services or the financial nobility who sell worthless mortgages. As an exploitable underclass, those who perform actual work have raised a vexing question for their superiors, and they seem to have fallen somewhat short of the right answer: How could they get the cheapest work out of their workers and still pay them enough to afford the products they have made? Though mere workers may be crippled by debt for their houses or farms or their children's education, they must still be able with some frequency to buy a new car or pickup truck or television set or motorboat or tractor or combine. If they have such things along with an occasional stunt in Outer Space, then maybe they won't covet a financial noble's private jet and three or four "homes."

Decades of cheap labor, cheap energy, and cheap food (all more expensive than has been imagined) have allowed our society to incorporate itself in a material structure that will have to be seen as topheavy. We have flooded the country, the roadsides and landfills, with shoddy "consumer goods." We have too many houses that are too big, too many public buildings that are gigantic, too much useless space enclosed in walls that are too high and under roofs that are too wide. We replaced an until-then-adequate system of railroads with an interstate highway system, expensive to build, disruptive of neighbor-hoods and local travel, increasingly expensive to maintain and use. We replaced an until-then-adequate system of local schools with con-solidated schools, letting the old buildings tumble down, replacing them with bigger ones, breaking the old ties between neighborhoods and schools, and making education entirely dependent on the fossil fuels. Every rural school now runs a fleet of buses for the underaged and provides a large parking lot for those over sixteen who "need" a car to go to school. Education has been oversold, overbuilt, over-electrified, and overpriced. Colleges have grown into universities. Universities have become "research institutions" full of undertaught students and highly accredited "professionals" who are overpaid by the public to job-train the young and to invent cures and solutions for corporations to "market" for too much money to the public. And we have balanced this immense superstructure, immensely expensive to use and maintain, upon the frail stem of the land economy that we conventionally abuse and ignore.

There is no good reason, economic or otherwise, to wish for the "recovery" and continuation of the economy we have had. There is no reason, really, to expect it to recover and continue, for it has depended too much on fantasy. An economy cannot "grow" forever on lim-ited resources. Energy and food cannot stay cheap forever. We can-not continue forever as a tax-dependent people who do not wish to pay taxes. Delusion and the future cannot serve forever as collateral. An untrustworthy economy dependent on trust cannot beguile the people's trust forever. The old props have been kicked away. The days when we could be safely crazy are over. Our airborne economy has turned into a deadfall, and we have got to jack it down. The problem is that all of us are under it, and so we have got to jack it down with the least possible suffering to our land and people. I don't know how this is to be done, and I am inclined to doubt that anybody does. You can't very confidently jack something down if you didn't know what you were doing when you jacked it up.

I do know that the human economy as a whole depends, as it always has, on nature and the land economy. The economy of land use is our link with nature. Though economic failure has not yet called any official attention to the land economy and its problems, those problems will have to be rightly solved if we are to solve rightly our other economic problems. Before we can make authentic solutions to the problems of credit and spending, we have got to begin by treating our land with the practical and effective love that alone deserves the name of patriotism. From now on, if we would like to continue here, our use of our land will have to be ruled by the principles of stewardship and thrift, using as the one indispensable measure, not monetary profit or industrial efficiency or professional success, but ecological health. And so I will venture to propose the following agenda of changes that would amount to a new, long-term agricultural policy:

1. There should be no further price supports or subsidies without production controls. This is because surplus production is an economic weapon, allowing corporations to reduce income to farmers while increasing their own income.

2. Return to 100 percent parity between agriculture and industry. Parity (fair) prices for agricultural products would make proposed payments for "ecological services" unnecessary, and would solve other problems as well.

3. Enforce anti-trust and anti-monopoly laws. Don't let *any* corporation get big, rich, or powerful enough to hold the nation for ransom. This applies with exceptional force to agribusiness and food corporations.

4. Help young farmers to own farms. In a sane economy such help would be unnecessary, but the departure of farm-raised young people from farming is now an agricultural crisis of the greatest urgency. And we don't have enough farm-raised young

people. Others need to be drawn in. Here are some measures we should consider. We should set appropriate and reasonable acreage limits, according to region, for family-scale farms and ranches. Taxes should be heavy on holdings above those limits. Holdings within the prescribed limits should be taxed at their agricultural value. There should be inheritance taxes on large holdings; none on small holdings. No-interest loans should be made available to young farmers and ranchers buying acreages under the limits. (These suggestions raise a lot of problems, and I flinch in making them. Acreage limits are hard to set appropriately, as we learned from the homestead laws. Also some of these measures would be unnecessary if land prices were not inflated above agricultural value, and if food prices were not deflated below their actual economic and ecological cost.

5. Phase out toxic chemicals, which are inconsistent with the principles of good agriculture, and which are polluting the rivers and the oceans.

6. Phase out biofuels as quickly as possible. We have got to observe a strict distinction between fire and food, driving and eating. We can't "feed the hungry" and feed automobiles from the same land, using the same land-destroying technologies and methods, forever.

7. Phase in perennial plants—for pasture, winter forage, and grain crops—to replace annual crops requiring annual soil disturbance or annual applications of "no-till" chemicals. This would bring a substantial reduction of soil erosion and toxicity.

8. Set and enforce high standards of water quality.

9. High water quality standards (enforced) and a program to replace annual crops with perennials would tend strongly toward the elimination of animal factories. But let us be forthright on this issue. We should get rid of animal factories, those abominations, as quickly as we can. Get the farm animals,

including hogs and chickens, back on grass. Put the animals where they belong, and their manure where it belongs.

10. Animal production should be returned to the scale of localities and communities. Do away with subsidies, incentives, and legislation favorable to gigantism in dairy, meat, and egg production.

11. Encourage the development of local food economies, which make more sense agriculturally and economically than our present overspecialized, too-concentrated, long-distance food economy. Local food economies are desirable also from the standpoints of public health, "homeland security," and the energy economy. Provide economic incentives and supportive legislation for the establishment of local, small-scale food-processing plants, canneries, year-round farmers' markets, etc.

12. Local food economies, to be genuine, require local adaptation of domestic species and varieties of plants and animals. The universal evolutionary requirement of local adaptation has unaccountably been waived with respect to humans. But this waiver is potentially disastrous. We need ways of agriculture that are preservingly adapted to the ecological mosaic and even to individual farms and ranches. For the sake of local adaptation, and the genetic diversity that is necessary to it, we need to put an end to the U.S. Department of Agriculture's proposed National Animal Identification System, to the patenting of species, and to genetic engineering—all of which aim at a general agricultural uniformity and corporate control of agriculture and food. Central planning and its inevitable goal of uniformity cannot work in agriculture because of the requirement of local adaptation and the consequent need for local intelligence. Central planning and uniformity are effective only for the diminishment of genetic and biological diversity and the destruction of small producers.

13. Help and encourage small-scale forestry and owners of small woodlands. See that current market prices for sawlogs and other forest products are readily available everywhere. Tax fairly.
14. Study and teach sustainable forestry, using examples such as the Menominee Forest in Wisconsin and the Pioneer Forest in Missouri.
15. Promote the good use and care of farm woodlands as assets integral to the economy of farms.
16. Encourage the development, in forested regions, of local forest economies, providing economic incentives for local processing and value-adding, as for food.

Would such measures increase significantly the number of people at work in the land economy? Of course they would. This would be an authentic version, for a change, of "job creation." This work would help our economy, our people, and our country all at the same time. And that is the authentic test of practicality, for it makes complete economic sense.

(2009)

Major in Homecoming

For Commencement, Northern Kentucky University

∞

Commencement speakers conventionally advise graduates that they must not think of the end of school as the end of education: They must continue to think of themselves as students and to study and learn for as long as they live.

I agree with that, as far as it goes, but it does not go far enough. I am now obliged to say to you graduates, not only that your education must continue, but also that it must change. It is necessary to say to you, moreover, that the institutions that so far have helped to educate you are going to have to change. As loyal alumni and responsible citizens, you are going to have to help them to change, even as you change yourselves.

I am taking the theme of this talk from my friend Wes Jackson of the Land Institute in Kansas, who has said, correctly, that our system of education until now has had only one major: Upward Mobility. Now, Wes says, a second major needs to be added, and the name of this major will be Homecoming.

The Upward Mobility major has put our schools far too much at the service of what we have been calling overconfidently our "economy." Education has increasingly been reduced to job training, preparing young people not for responsible adulthood and citizenship but for expert servitude to the corporations. There has been an ongoing feeble objection to this reduction, but most people have been willing to ignore or tolerate it, or even applaud it, despite the obvious dangers. Now, however, the failure of the economy and its subservient institutions has become too obvious to be denied. We are now facing a hardship long deferred. We have no choice but to do better.

That our economy has been enormously destructive has been evident for many years, and nowhere has this been more evident than here in Kentucky. The occupation of this state by people predominantly European began 234 years ago. In so brief a time we have destroyed or blighted or used up a far greater fraction of the state's natural bounty than good care for as many years could restore. Most of this damage has been done, and at an ever-accelerating rate, during my lifetime. Much of what we have destroyed is gone forever. The fossil fuels that we have so regardlessly extracted and burned cannot be unburned. The topsoils and forests and watersheds destroyed by mining will not be replenished in a time imaginable by humans. Virtually all of the original forest is long gone, and much of the regrowth has been abusively logged. Virtually all of our streams are polluted, and we are contributing our share to the pollution of the earth's atmosphere. Erosion has carried away immense tonnages of soil from our farms and woodlands, which are increasingly threatened also by invasive plants, insects, and diseases. All this we have so far accepted as normal effects of our economy. But at present rates of use and abuse, it is impossible to suppose that our state will remain inhabitable for another hundred years. We have tried—or tried again—the experiment of building urban prosperity by the impoverishment of the countryside and its people, and inevitably we have failed. The result has been impoverishment that is both rural and urban.

Now we have seen that this economy, which has "externalized" so many and such extreme costs to our land and people, is on its own terms a failure. It is not, in fact, in any respectable sense an economy, but rather a financial system based on easy credit, cheap energy, over-consumption, unsupportable "development," waste, fantasy, "bubbles," and sometimes on nothing at all. It is now undeniable—though some will attempt to deny it—that we are involved deeply and intricately in an economic disaster, in which the production of monetary wealth involves the destruction of necessary goods. Even if the climate were ideal and perfectly stable—even if we had an inexhaustible supply of cheap, portable, nonpolluting fuel—our present economic assumptions and practices would ruin us. Upward mobility, as we now are seeing, implies downward mobility, just as it has always implied lateral mobility. It implies, in fact, social instability, ecological oblivion, and economic insecurity.

To have founded an enormously expensive system of education on the premises of, and in service to, such an economy has been a mistake, calling for a long, arduous work of revision. If authentic hope is to survive in our present circumstances, education will have to change, and by "education" I mean both self-education and the work of schools. "After all," wrote the great Canadian ecologist Stan Rowe, "well-educated people, not illiterates, are wrecking the planet. Schools and universities are morally bankrupt [and] most research is worthless busywork..." I would add that some research is worse than worthless; it contributes directly to the wrecking of the planet.

The change that is called for is a shift from the economy to the ecosphere as the basis of curriculum, teaching, and learning. That is because the ecosphere is inescapably the basis and context of any possible economy. The proper goal of education, according to Stan Rowe, is "understanding what it means to be human in a living world." He says further that "we should be asking how the things we construct . . . connect us to the enveloping Ecosphere. . . . Do they love the ground on which they stand?" He calls our attention to "the process whereby organisms get established in place, making themselves partners with air, soil, water and other organisms."

This process, for humans as for all other living creatures, is local adaptation. We know that local adaptation is a necessity for the survival of all species: They either adapt to their places, or they die. How is it that our learned teachers and researchers have exempted our own species from this stark choice?

If schools will not prepare students for this choice—or for this process of local adaptation that Wes Jackson appropriately calls homecoming—then their graduates will have to acquire such an education for themselves. But eventually the schools, and their students, and their graduates, are going to see that homecoming is not an elective. It is a requirement. We could call it Emergency Ecological Training.

Such an education will require acceptance of locality—what Stan Rowe called "home place"—as the context of study, thought, and work. This in turn will require humility, a virtue not encouraged or esteemed by the modern arts and sciences. But the major in homecoming will not make us intellectual heroes. It will begin, and end, with a confession of ignorance. For we all are ignorant in varying degrees of where we are, of what we need to do to stay there, of what we need to do to assure that our children and grandchildren can stay there. And so the homecoming curriculum will be a curriculum of questions such as the following:

1. What has happened here? By "here" I mean wherever you live and work.

2. What should have happened here?
3. What is here now? What is left of the original natural endowment? What has been lost? What has been added?
4. What is the nature, or genius, of this place?
5. What will nature permit us to do here without permanent damage or loss?
6. What will nature help us to do here?
7. What can we do to mend the damages we have done?
8. What are the limits: Of the nature of this place? Of our intelligence and ability?

Obviously, these questions cannot be answered—and they are not likely to be asked—by a specialist, or by many specialists working in isolation. They *can* be asked, and eventually answered to a significant extent, by a conversation across the disciplinary boundaries. This would not be a conversation with a foreseeable, or even a possible, end. It would be carried on necessarily in the face of forever changing conditions and circumstances, leading to further revelations of ignorance, and thus to necessary refinements or changes in the agenda of questions.

This conversation would collapse the rigidly departmented structure of our present academic and professional system into a vital, wakeful society of local communities elegantly adapted to local ecosystems.

If this conversation ever should take place in our schools, academic life would be jolted out of the doldrums of "the industrial model" into a new birth of freedom and purpose. Teaching then could resume its old sense of neighborly duty and responsibility. Research might rise above commercial and professional preoccupations and achieve the dignity of honorable study—study, this time, serving the survival of species, including our own.

You graduates will have to work for such a change in the schools for the sake of generations to come. But you also will have to work for such a change in yourselves, reading and conversing and living across the disciplinary boundaries, for your own sake, for the sake of your own homecoming. This effort has already been started for you by the many people all over our country, and all over the world, who are working for local economies that are authentically conserving. Beyond its benefit to the survival of a good, beautiful, and livable world, this work of homecoming has a lot to recommend it. It is endlessly interesting, and endlessly productive of decent, undamaging pleasures.

(2009)

The Love of Farming

∞

I read Louis Bromfield's *Pleasant Valley* and *The Farm* more than forty years ago, and I am still grateful for the confirmation and encouragement I received from those books. At a time when farming, as a vocation and an art, was going out of favor, Louis Bromfield was a writer who genuinely and unabashedly loved it. This love was not that of bad pastoral writers whose love is distant, sentimental, and condescending. Bromfield clearly had loved it familiarly and in detail; he loved the work and the people who did it well.

In any discussion of agriculture or food production, it would be hard to exaggerate the importance of such love. No doubt there are people who farm without it, but without it nobody will be a good farmer or a good husbander of the land. We seem now to be coming to a time when we will have to recognize the love of farming, not as a quaint souvenir of an outdated past, but as an economic necessity.

And that recognition, when it comes, will bring with it a considerable embarrassment.

How great an embarrassment this may be is suggested by a recent article in the *Wall Street Journal* about Japan's effort to "job-train" unemployed urban young people to be farmers. This is a serious effort, even an urgent one. "Policy makers," the article says, "are hoping newly unemployed young people will help revive Japan's dwindling farm population . . . 'If they can't find workers over the next several years, Japan's agriculture will disappear,' says Kazumasa Iwata, a government economist and former deputy governor of the Bank of Japan." But this effort is falling significantly short of success, because "many young people end up returning to cities, unable to adjust to life in the countryside." To their surprise, evidently, farming involves hard work, long hours, and getting dirty—not to mention skills that city-bred people don't have. Not to mention the necessity to love farm work if you are going to keep at it.

Even so, the prospect for reviving agriculture in Japan is brighter than in the United States. In Japan 6 percent of the population is still farming, as opposed to maybe 1 percent of our people. And in Japan, as opposed to the United States, policy makers and economists seem to be aware of the existence of agriculture. They even think that agriculture may be a good thing for a nation of eaters to have.

If agriculture and the necessity of food production ever penetrate the consciousness of our politicians and economists, how successful will they be in job-training our overeducated, ignorant young people to revive our own aging and dwindling farm population? What will it take to get significant numbers of our young people, white of collar and soft of hands, to submit to hard work and long days, let alone to getting dirty? In my worst, clearest moments I am afraid the necessity of agriculture will not be widely recognized apart from the sterner necessity of actual hunger. For half a century or so, our informal but most effective agricultural policy has been to eat as much, as effortlessly, as thoughtlessly, and as cheaply as we can, to hell with whatever else may be involved. Such a policy can of course lead to actual hunger.

In Goethe's *Faust*, the devil Mephistopheles is fulfilling some of the learned doctor's wishes by means of witchcraft, which the doctor is finding unpleasant. The witches cook up a brew that promises to make him young, but Faust is nauseated by it. He asks (this is Randall Jarrell's translation):

> *Has neither Nature nor some noble mind*
> *Discovered some remedy, some balsam?*

Mephistopheles, who is a truth-telling devil, replies:

> *There is a natural way to make you young . . .*
> > *Go out in a field*
> *And start right in to work: dig, hoe,*
> *Keep your thoughts and yourself in that field,*
> *Eat the food you raise . . .*
> *Be willing to manure the field you harvest.*
> *And that's the best way—take it from me! —*
> *To go on being young at eighty.*

Faust, a true intellectual, unsurprisingly objects:

> *Oh, but to live spade in hand—*
> *I'm not used to it, I couldn't stand it.*
> *So narrow a life would not suit me.*

And Mephistopheles replies:

> *Well then, we still must have the witch.*

Lately I've been returning to that passage again and again, and every time I read it I laugh. I laugh because it is a piece of superb wit, and because it is true. Faust's idea that farm life is necessarily "narrow" remains perfectly up-to-date. It is still true that to escape that alleged narrowness requires the agency of a supra-natural or extra-human power—though now, for Goethe's witchcraft, we would properly substitute industrial agriculture.

This progress from witchcraft to industrial agriculture does not seem to be especially happy. We could be forgiven, I think, if we find it horrifying. Farming does involve working hard and getting dirty. Faust, perhaps understandably, does not love it. To escape it, for a while at least, he has only to drink a nauseating beverage concocted by witches. But we, who have decided as a nation and by policy not to love farming, have escaped it, for a while at least, by turning it into an "agri-industry." But agri-industry is a package containing far more than its label confesses. In addition to an array of labor-saving or people-replacing devices and potions, it has given us massive soil erosion and degradation, water pollution, maritime hypoxic zones, destroyed rural communities and cultures, a farming population dwindled almost to disappearance, toxic food, and an absolute dependence on a despised and exploited force of migrant workers.

This is not, by any accounting, a bargain. Maybe we have begun to see that it is not, but we have only begun. As a nation, we have ahead of us a lot of hard work that we are not going to be able to do with clean hands. We had better try to love it.

(2009)

Faustian Economics

∞

The general reaction to the apparent end of the era of cheap fossil fuel, as to other readily foreseeable curtailments, has been to delay any sort of reckoning. The strategies of delay, so far, have been a sort of willed oblivion, or visions of large profits to the manufacturers of such "biofuels" as ethanol from corn or switchgrass, or the familiar unscientific faith that "science will find an answer." The dominant response, in short, is a dogged belief that what we call "the American way of life" will prove somehow indestructible. We will keep on consuming, spending, wasting, and driving, as before, at any cost to anything and everybody but ourselves.

This belief was always indefensible—the real names of global warming are "waste" and "greed"—and by now it is manifestly foolish. But foolishness on this scale looks disturbingly like a sort of national insanity. We seem to have come to a collective delusion of grandeur, insisting that all of us are "free" to be as conspicuously greedy and wasteful as the most corrupt of kings and queens. (Perhaps by devoting more and more of our already abused cropland to fuel production, we will at last cure ourselves of obesity and become fashionably skeletal, hungry but—Thank God!—still driving.)

The problem with us is not only prodigal extravagance, but also an assumed godly limitlessness. We have obscured the issue by refusing to see that limitlessness is a godly trait. We have insistently, and with relief, defined ourselves as animals or as "higher animals." But to define ourselves as animals, given our specifically human powers and desires, is to define ourselves as *limitless* animals—which of course is a contradiction in terms. Any definition is a limit, which is why the God of Exodus refuses to define Himself: "I am that I am."

Even so, that we have founded our present society upon delusional assumptions of limitlessness is easy enough to demonstrate. A recent "summit" in Louisville, Kentucky, was entitled "Unbridled Energy: The Industrialization of Kentucky's Energy Resources." Its subjects were "clean-coal generation, biofuels, and other cutting-edge applications," the conversion of coal to "liquid fuels," and the likelihood that all this will be "environmentally friendly." These hopes, which "can create jobs and boost the nation's security," are to be supported by government "loan guarantees ... investment tax credits and other tax breaks." Such talk we recognize as completely conventional. It is, in fact, a tissue of clichés that is now the common tongue of promoters, politicians, and journalists. This language does not allow for any question about the *net* good of anything proposed. The entire contraption of "Unbridled Energy" is supported only by a rote optimism: "The United States has 250 billion tons of recoverable coal reserves— enough to last 100 years even at double the current rate of consumption." [1] We humans have inhabited the earth for many thousands of years, and now we can look forward to surviving for another hundred by doubling our consumption of coal? *This* is national security? The

world-ending fire of industrial fundamentalism may already be burning in our furnaces and engines, but if it will burn for a hundred more
years, that will be fine. Surely it would be better to intend straight-
forwardly to contain the fire and eventually put it out? But once
greed has been made an honorable motive, then you have an economy
without limits, a contradiction in terms. This supposed economy has
no plan for temperance or thrift or the ecological law of return. It will
do anything. It is monstrous by definition.*

In keeping with our unrestrained consumptiveness, the commonly
accepted basis of our present economy is the fantastical possibility
of limitless growth, limitless wants, limitless wealth, limitless natural
resources, limitless energy, and limitless debt. The idea of a limitless
economy implies and requires a doctrine of general human limitlessness: *All* are entitled to pursue without limit whatever they conceive
as desirable—a license that classifies the most exalted Christian capitalist with the lowliest pornographer.

This fantasy of limitlessness perhaps arose from the coincidence of
the industrial revolution with the suddenly exploitable resources of
the "new world." Or perhaps it comes from the contrary apprehen-
sion of the world's "smallness," made possible by modern astronomy
and high-speed transportation. Fear of the smallness of our world
and its life may lead to a kind of claustrophobia and thence, with
apparent reasonableness, to a desire for the "freedom" of limitlessness.
But this desire paradoxically reduces everything. The life of this world
is small to those who think it is, and the desire to enlarge it makes it
smaller, and can reduce it finally to nothing.

However it came about, this credo of limitlessness clearly implies a
principled wish, not only for limitless possessions, but also for limitless knowledge, limitless science, limitless technology, and limitless

---

* This is abundantly demonstrated by the suddenly ubiquitous rationalizations of
"clean" and "safe" nuclear energy, ignoring the continuing problem of undisposable
waste.

progress. And necessarily it must lead to limitless violence, waste, war, and destruction. That it should finally produce a crowning cult of political limitlessness is only a matter of mad logic.

The normalization of the doctrine of limitlessness has produced a sort of moral minimalism: the desire to be "efficient" at any cost, to be unencumbered by complexity. The minimization of neighborliness, respect, reverence, responsibility, accountability, and self-subordination—this is the "culture" of which our present leaders and heroes are the spoiled children.

Our national faith so far has been "There's always more." Our true religion is a sort of autistic industrialism. People of intelligence and ability seem now to be genuinely embarrassed by any solution to any problem that does not involve high technology, a great expenditure of energy, or a big machine. Thus an X marked on a paper ballot no longer fulfills our idea of voting. One problem with this state of affairs is that the work now most needing to be done—that of neighborliness and caretaking—cannot be done by remote control with the greatest power on the largest scale. A second problem is that the economic fantasy of limitlessness in a limited world calls fearfully into question the value of our monetary wealth, which does not reliably stand for the real wealth of land, resources, and workmanship, but instead wastes and depletes it.

That human limitlessness is a fantasy means, obviously, that its life expectancy is limited. There is now a growing perception, and not just among a few experts, that we are entering a time of inescapable limits. We are not likely to be granted another world to plunder in compensation for our pillage of this one. Nor are we likely to believe much longer in our ability to outsmart, by means of science and technology, our economic stupidity. The hope that we can cure the ills of industrialism by the homeopathy of more technology seems at last to be losing status. We are, in short, coming under pressure to understand ourselves as limited creatures in a limited world.

This constraint, however, is not the condemnation it may seem. On the contrary, it returns us to our real condition and to our human heritage, from which our self-definition as limitless animals has for too long cut us off. Every cultural and religious tradition that I know about, while fully acknowledging our animal nature, defines us specifically as *humans*—that is, as animals (if the word still applies) capable of living, not only within natural limits, but also within cultural limits, self-imposed. As earthly creatures we live, because we must, within natural limits, which we may describe by such names as "earth" or "ecosystem" or "watershed" or "place" or "neighborhood." But as humans we may elect to respond to this necessary placement by the self-restraints implied in neighborliness, stewardship, thrift, temperance, generosity, care, kindness, friendship, loyalty, and love.

In our limitless selfishness, we have tried to define "freedom," for example, as an escape from all restraint. But, as my friend Bert Hornback has explained in his book *The Wisdom in Words*, "free" is etymologically related to "friend." These words come from the same Germanic and Sanskrit roots, which carry the sense of "dear" or "beloved." [2] We set our friends free by our love for them, with the implied restraints of faithfulness or loyalty. This suggests that our "identity" is located not in the impulse of selfhood but in deliberately maintained connections.

Thinking of our predicament has sent me back again to Christopher Marlowe's *Tragical History of Doctor Faustus*. This is a play of the Renaissance: Faustus, a man of learning, longs to possess "all nature's treasury," to "Ransack the ocean . . . / And search all corners of the new-found world . . ." [3] To assuage his thirst for knowledge and power, he deeds his soul to Lucifer, receiving in compensation for twenty-four years the services of the subdevil Mephistophilis, nominally his slave but in fact his master. Having the subject of limitlessness in mind, I was astonished on this reading to come upon Mephistophilis' description of hell. When Faustus asks, "How comes it then that thou art out of hell?" Mephistophilis replies, "Why, this is hell, nor am I out of it."[4] A few pages later he explains:

> *Hell hath no limits, nor is circumscribed*
> *In one self place, but where we [the damned] are is hell,*
> *And where hell is must we ever be.*[5]

For those who reject heaven, hell is everywhere, and thus is limitless. For them, even the thought of heaven is hell.

It is only appropriate, then, that Mephistophilis rejects any conventional limit: "Tut, Faustus, marriage is but a ceremonial toy. If thou lovest me, think no more of it."[6] Continuing this theme, for Faustus' pleasure the devils present a sort of pageant of the seven deadly sins, three of which—Pride, Wrath, and Gluttony—describe themselves as orphans, disdaining the restraints of parental or filial love.

Seventy or so years later, and with the issue of the human definition more than ever in doubt, John Milton in Book VII of *Paradise Lost* returns again to a consideration of our urge to know. To Adam's request to be told the story of creation, the "affable Archangel" Raphael agrees "to answer thy desire / Of knowledge *within bounds* [my emphasis] . . . ,"[7] explaining that

> *Knowledge is as food, and needs no less*
> *Her temperance over appetite, to know*
> *In measure what the mind may well contain;*
> *Oppresses else with surfeit, and soon turns*
> *Wisdom to folly, as nourishment to wind.*[8]

Raphael is saying, with angelic circumlocution, that knowledge without wisdom, limitless knowledge, is not worth a fart; he is not a humorless archangel. But he also is saying that knowledge without measure, knowledge that the human mind cannot appropriately use, is mortally dangerous.

I am well aware of what I risk in bringing this language of religion into what is normally a scientific discussion—if economics is in fact a science. I do so because I doubt that we can define our present problems adequately, let alone solve them, without some recourse to our cultural heritage. We are, after all, trying now to deal with the failure of scientists, technicians, and politicians to "think up" a version of human continuance that is economically probable and ecologically responsible, or perhaps even imaginable. If we go back into our tradition, we are going to find a concern with religion, which at a minimum shatters the selfish context of the individual life and thus forces a consideration of what human beings are and ought to be.

This concern persists at least as late as our Declaration of Independence, which holds as "self-evident, that all men are created equal; that they are endowed by their Creator with certain inalienable rights ..." Thus among our political roots we have still our old preoccupation with our definition as humans, which in the Declaration is wisely assigned to our Creator; our rights and the rights of all humans are not granted by any human government but are innate, belonging to us by birth. This insistence comes, not from the fear of death or even extinction, but from the ancient fear, readily documentable in our cultural tradition, that in order to survive we might become inhuman or monstrous.

Our cultural tradition is in large part the record of our continuing effort to understand ourselves as beings specifically human—to say that, as humans, we must do certain things and we must not do certain things. We must have limits or we will cease to exist as humans; perhaps we will cease to exist, period. At times, for example, some of us humans have thought that human beings, properly so-called, did not make war against civilian populations, or hold prisoners without a fair trial, or use torture for any reason.

Some of us would-be humans have thought too that we should not be free at anybody else's expense. And yet in the phrase "free market," the word "free" has come to mean unlimited economic power for some, with the necessary consequence of economic powerlessness for others. Several years ago, after I had spoken at a meeting, two earnest and obviously troubled young veterinarians approached me with a question: How could they practice veterinary medicine without serious economic damage to the farmers who were their clients? Underlying their question was the fact that for a long time veterinary help for a sheep or a pig has been likely to cost more than the animal is worth. I had to answer that, in my opinion, so long as their practice relied heavily on selling patented drugs, they had no choice, since the market for medicinal drugs was entirely controlled by the drug companies, whereas most farmers had no control at all over the market for agricultural products. My questioners were asking in effect if a predatory economy can have a beneficent result. The answer usually is No. And that is because there is an absolute discontinuity between the economy of the seller of medicines and the economy of the buyer, as there is in the health industry as a whole. The drug industry is interested in the survival of patients, we have to suppose, because surviving patients will continue to consume drugs.

Now let us consider a contrary example. Recently at another meeting I talked for some time with an elderly, some would say old-fashioned, farmer from Nebraska. Unable to farm any longer himself, he had rented his land to a younger farmer on the basis of what he called "crop share" instead of a price paid or owed in advance. Thus, as the old farmer said of his renter, "If he has a good year, I have a good year. If he has a bad year, I have a bad one." This is what I would call community economy. It is a sharing of fate. It assures an economic continuity and a common interest between the two partners to the trade. This is as far as possible from the economy in which the young veterinarians were caught, in which the economically powerful are limitlessly "free" to trade to the disadvantage, and ultimately the ruin, of the powerless.

It is this economy of community destruction that, wittingly or unwittingly, most scientists and technicians have served for the last two hundred years. These scientists and technicians have justified themselves by the proposition that they are the vanguard of progress, enlarging human knowledge and power. Thus have they romanticized both themselves and the predatory enterprises that they have served.

As a consequence, our great need now is for sciences and technologies of limits, of domesticity, of what Wes Jackson of the Land Institute in Salina, Kansas, has called "homecoming." These would be specifically human sciences and technologies, working, as the best humans always have worked, within self-imposed limits. The limits would be, as they always have been, the accepted contexts of places, communities, and neighborhoods, both natural and human.

I know that the idea of such limitations will horrify some people, maybe most people, for we have long encouraged ourselves to feel at home on "the cutting edges" of knowledge and power or on some "frontier" of human experience. But I know too that we are talking now in the presence of much evidence that improvement by outward expansion may no longer be a good idea, if it ever was. It was not a good idea for the farmers who "leveraged" secure acreage to buy more during the 1970s. It has proved tragically to be a bad idea in a number of recent wars. If it is a good idea in the form of corporate gigantism, then we must ask, For whom? Faustus, who wants all knowledge and all the world for himself, is a man supremely lonely and finally doomed. I don't think Marlowe was kidding. I don't think Satan is kidding when he says in *Paradise Lost*, "myself am Hell." [9]

If the idea of appropriate limitation seems unacceptable to us, that may be because, like Marlowe's Faustus and Milton's Satan, we confuse limits with confinement. But that, as I think Marlowe and Milton and others were trying to tell us, is a great and potentially a fatal mistake. Satan's fault, as Milton understood it and perhaps with some sympathy, was precisely that he could not tolerate his proper limitation; he could not subordinate himself to anything whatsoever. Faustus' error was his unwillingness to remain "Faustus, and a man."[10] In our age of the world it is not rare to find writers, critics, and teachers of literature, as well as scientists and technicians, who regard Satan's and Faustus' defiance as salutary and heroic.

On the contrary, our human and earthly limits, properly understood, are not confinements, but rather are inducements to formal elaboration and elegance, to *fullness* of relationship and meaning. Perhaps our most serious cultural loss in recent centuries is the knowledge that some things, though limited, can be inexhaustible. For example, an ecosystem, even that of a working forest or farm, so long as it remains ecologically intact, is inexhaustible. A small place, as I know from my own experience, can provide opportunities of work and learning, and a fund of beauty, solace, and pleasure—in addition to its difficulties—that cannot be exhausted in a lifetime or in generations.

To recover from our disease of limitlessness, we will have to give up the idea that we have a right to be godlike animals, that we are at least potentially omniscient and omnipotent, ready to discover "the secret of the universe." We will have to start over, with a different and much older premise: the naturalness and, for creatures of limited intelligence, the necessity of limits. We must learn again to ask how we can make the most of what we are, what we have, what we have been given. If we always have a theoretically better substitute available from somebody or someplace else, we will never make the most of anything. It is hard enough to make the most of one life. If we each had two lives, we would not make much of either. One of my best teachers said of people in general: "They'll never be worth a damn as long as they've got two choices."

To deal with the problems, which after all are inescapable, of living with limited intelligence in a limited world, I suggest that we may have to remove some of the emphasis we have lately placed on science and technology and have a new look at the arts. For an art does not propose to enlarge itself by limitless extension, but rather to enrich itself within bounds that are accepted prior to the work.

It is the artists, not the scientists, who have dealt unremittingly with the problem of limits. A painting, however large, must finally be bounded by a frame or a wall. A composer or playwright must reckon, at a minimum, with the capacity of an audience to sit still and pay attention. A story, once begun, must end somewhere within the limits of the writer's and the reader's memory. And of course the arts characteristically impose limits that are artificial: the five acts of a play, or the fourteen lines of a sonnet. Within these limits artists achieve elaborations of pattern, of sustaining relationships of parts with one another and with the whole, that may be astonishingly complex. Probably most of us can name a painting, a piece of music, a poem or play or story that still grows in meaning and remains fresh after many years of familiarity.

We know by now that a natural ecosystem survives by the same sort of formal intricacy, ever-changing, inexhaustible, and perhaps finally unknowable. We know further that if we want to make our economic landscapes sustainably and abundantly productive, we must do so by maintaining in them a living formal complexity something like that of natural ecosystems. We can do this only by raising to the highest level our mastery of the arts of agriculture, animal husbandry, forestry, and, ultimately, the art of living.

It is true that insofar as scientific experiments must be conducted within carefully observed limits, scientists also are artists. But in science one experiment, whether it succeeds or fails, is logically followed by another in a theoretically infinite progression. According to the underlying myth of modern science, this progression is always replacing the smaller knowledge of the past with the larger knowledge of the present, which will be replaced by the yet larger knowledge of the future.

In the arts, by contrast, no limitless sequence of works is ever implied or looked for. No work of art is necessarily followed by a second work that is necessarily better. Given the methodologies of science, the law of gravity and the genome were bound to be discovered by somebody; the identity of the discoverer is incidental. But in the arts there are no second chances. We must assume that we had one chance each for *The Divine Comedy* and *King Lear*. If Dante and Shakespeare had died before they wrote those poems, nobody ever would have written them.

The same is true of our arts of land use, our economic arts, which are our arts of living. With these it is once-for-all. We will have no chance to redo our experiments with bad agriculture leading to soil loss. The Appalachian mountains and forests we have destroyed for coal are gone forever. It is now and forevermore too late to use thriftily the first half of the world's supply of petroleum. In the art of living we can only start again with what remains.

As we confront the phenomenon of "peak oil," we are really confronting the end of our customary delusion of "more." Whichever way we turn, from now on, we are going to find a limit beyond which there will be no more. To hit these limits at top speed is not a rational choice. To start slowing down, with the idea of avoiding catastrophe, *is* a rational choice, and a viable one if we can recover the necessary political sanity. Of course it makes sense to consider alternative energy sources, provided *they* make sense. But also we will have to reexamine

the economic structures of our life, and conform them to the toler-
ances and limits of our earthly places. Where there is no more, our
one choice is to make the most and the best of what we have.

(2006)

NOTES

1 *Louisville Courier-Journal*, October 21, 2006.
2 Bert Hornback, *The Wisdom in Words* (Louisville: Bellarmine University Press,
   2010), 10.
3 Marlowe, *The Tragical History of Doctor Faustus*, scene 1, lines 77, 85-86.
4 Ibid., scene 3, line 77.
5 Ibid., scene 5, lines 123-25.
6 Ibid., scene 5, lines 152-53.
7 Milton, *Paradise Lost*, bk. 7, lines 119-20.
8 Ibid., bk. 7, lines 126-30.
9 Ibid., bk. 4, line 75.
10 Ibid., bk. 1, line 23.

Simple Solutions, Package Deals, and a 50-Year Farm Bill

∞

As our economy has been showing us for the past year or so, we have become a nation of fantasists. With a kind of abject credulity, we have come to believe in the power of money alone to bring forth goods, to believe that money itself *is* a good, to believe that consumption is as vital an economic activity as production. We think that shopping is a patriotic act and a public service. We tolerate fabulous capitalists who think a bet on a debt is an asset.

It is becoming harder to remember—especially, it seems, for most economists—that our lives depend upon the economies of land use, and that the land-using economies depend, in turn, on the ecosphere. It is nonetheless a fact that we cannot have life or health or wealth apart from the health of the natural world—of land, water, and air. A further and more demanding fact is that land, water, and air cannot be healthful apart from a healthful human economy, beginning with farming, forestry, and mining.

Mining we have allowed to become an industrial war against the land and all its living communities, taking whatever is of most immediate value, and leaving in return ruins and poisons that are substantially worse than nothing. Perhaps it is not surprising that, ignorant and indifferent as we are, we have allowed the economies of agriculture and forestry to mimic the economy of mining, making potentially renewable and sustainable resources nonrenewable, taking much temporary wealth and returning permanent ruin to the land and its natural and human communities.

A nation skilled and educated in fantasy is going to have trouble understanding, and so is going to resist understanding, that healthful land-use economies are immediately complex and ultimately mysterious—and that healthful ecosystems, on which healthful land-use economies depend, are immediately even more complex and ultimately even more mysterious. We like to believe that all choices are simple, as between an obvious good and an obvious evil, as between two silverware patterns or two automobiles. But in the economies of land use there are no simple choices, and no consequences that do not ramify perhaps endlessly. The results of such choices are not limited, not linear, but are intricately and at last mysteriously formal.

Back in the 1970s, with the examples of good Amish farms before us, my friend Maurice Telleen of the *Draft Horse Journal* helped me to see that the presence of draft horses or mules on those farms was not a simple choice of one kind of traction power over another. It was instead a choice of one kind of farming, and one way of thinking about farming, over another. What Maury understood and helped me to understand was that those work animals were a determining force against specialization and for diversity. They were part of a package or a pattern. If you were working horses or mules, then, merely in the

nature of things and following an obvious logic, you would also have
pastures, forage crops, fenced fields, feed grains, and barns for stable
room and feed storage. Those things in turn made for the keeping of
other kinds of animals. Diversity of crops and animals led, in turn,
to the rotation of crops, the use of cover crops, the use of manure as
fertilizer. The farm thus sponsored much of its own operating energy
and fertility. Moreover, the use of draft animals determined the scale
of the farm. The farms had to be what we would call "small" or "family-
sized"—acreages that could be worked and maintained with a reasonable expenditure of effort by the work animals and therefore by
the people as well. A good Amish farmer told me that he had learned
from his father never to have a horse harnessed after supper. That
amenity guaranteed enough rest and good health for the horses, and
also some needed leisure for the family.

If the use of draft animals implies diversity, homegrown energy
and fertility, appropriateness of scale, and a significant measure of
built-in economic health on the farm, it also implies economic diversity and health in the local community. I am thinking, for example,
of Holmes County, Ohio, where the horse-powered farms are sup-
plied and served by an impressive variety of local shops, trades, and
industries: harness makers, farriers, family-run farm equipment factories, and so on. I am also thinking of the small towns of my boyhood, in which all sorts of independent small businesses survived
and even thrived by participating in an economy of small, horse- or
mule-powered farms—in which shoe-repair shops repaired harness,
and a lot of farm equipment was built or rebuilt or repaired in local
blacksmith shops.

If we can see that draft animals on the farm belonged to and led to
a distinctive kind of farming, then we will have no trouble in seeing
that the substitution of tractors for draft animals belonged to and
led to farming of a radically different kind. The tractors too have

proved to be part of a package, as now we can see. The tractor package included increased dependence on farm equipment corporations and oil companies, increased dependence on credit, increased dependence on toxic chemicals, ever-larger farms and ever fewer farmers, loss of diversity, increased specialization, more acres planted in annual crops and fewer in perennials, more soil erosion, clearing of woodlots, removal of fences and fencerows, less diversity both domestic and wild. All this implies and has led to a highly centralized long-distance food economy, and a commensurate decline of local economies and communities and of the whole social structure of rural America. And obviously you cannot disrupt the social structure of the countryside without disrupting the social structure of the cities.

About now I begin to hear the distant rumble of two accusations that experience has taught me to anticipate: namely, that I am trying to "turn back the clock," and that I am a Luddite.

Well, I certainly am not trying to turn back the clock. I know, for example, that we cannot recover the topsoil that we have squandered since we began to impose our extractive, persistently colonialist economy on the so-called New World. I know we cannot recover our rural communities and local farming cultures, such as they were, flawed as they were, before 1950. We have no place to start but where we are, which is not news, but merely the truth. We do need to have some authentic understanding of the choices we have made.

On the other hand, I am indeed a Luddite, if by that I may mean that I would not willingly see my community—to the extent that I still have one—destroyed by any technological innovation. Most present-day farmers are, for a number of reasons, not capable of choosing to farm with horses, and so there would be little use in suggesting to them that they can't farm well with tractors. They can, and many do, but to do so they must measure and regulate their work by the nature, the carrying capacity, and the sustaining pattern of their farms, not by the capabilities of the available machines.

Though there is no contest, at present, between draft animals and tractors, I don't want to neglect to say that there is at present a well-started and ongoing contest between creatures and machines, and in this contest the creatures have good reason to worry.

The same interests and forces that have brought about our centralized, long-distance agricultural economy have also brought about a centralized, long-distance forest economy. The economic principle is everywhere the same: a domestic colonialism that extracts an immense wealth from our rural landscapes, returning as near nothing as possible or nothing or worse than nothing to the land and the people. The producers of agricultural products, nearly all, nearly always, are at the mercy of the market and the buyers. Producers of forest products are in the same fix.

Given the growing demand for local food, and the increasing numbers of farmers' markets and Community Supported Agriculture farms, it is becoming possible to imagine the development of local farm and food economies in which communities and localities produce, process, market, and consume local farm products, marketing any surpluses to outside demand.

But we need to be moving also toward the integration of forestry into the local farm and food economy, wherever the farms are likely to include woodlands. Wherever forests or woodlands are predominant in the landscape, we need to think of developing local forest economies that, instead of exporting raw logs, would produce, process or manufacture, and market the fullest variety of forest products, from lumber for building to mushrooms and nuts, from fenceposts to firewood, from Christmas decorations to finished furniture.

The answer, the only answer, to economic colonialism is to make the greatest local advantage of the products of the local countryside, producing and processing for local consumption first of all, and only then for export. This exactly reverses the colonial economy that, if it could, would have the local people starve in order to export food, or live in shacks and shanties in order to export logs. In the Appalachian coal fields a colonial economy does in fact cause the local people to live in severely and dangerously degraded landscapes to enable the export of coal.

Obviously, in talking about the development of local economies based on local products, I am giving an improved sense to that weary phrase "job creation." If your community is making its living primarily by the export of raw materials for manufacture elsewhere, then along with your logs or your wheat or your cattle or your minerals you are exporting jobs, and then you will be exporting your young people to take those jobs. All that is clear enough. We have seen it happening.

Perhaps the most important point in favor of local economy is that by making an economy local we necessarily make it diverse. That is because local needs are diverse. If we attempt to make our versatile landscapes as responsive as possible to the diversity of local needs, then we would be solving, not one, but many problems.

This of course would be contrary to the economic tendency of our country, especially in recent times. Our tendency has been to fasten upon one local product, and allow that one to determine the local land economy. One reason I don't long to turn back the clock is that I don't know a time that I would like to turn the clock back to. Even so, we have made choices and changes, and we need to think critically of our history. I remember a way of farming here in Kentucky that was comparatively diverse and at best well structured, farm by farm. I remember when Louisville lived, to a significant extent, from its surrounding landscape. I remember excellent sheep flocks and herds of cattle on beautifully maintained Central Kentucky farms that were not horse farms. I remember when most farm families subsisted primarily from their own land and home economies. These memories don't tell me that I once lived in an ideal age, above criticism. They

tell me that by now we have become too much determined by outside influence and too little self-determining; too concentrated, too
specialized, and too vulnerable; too thoughtless or neglectful of good
possibilities in our land and people.

The economic advantages of diverse local land-based economies
such as I am talking about are clear enough. Their promise is not
luxury or extravagance for a few, but a modest, decent, sustainable
prosperity for many. In addition, there would be an equally significant
ecological advantage. In a complex local economy, in which a lot of
people were economically dependent on the products of the local
landscape, there would be the strongest local support for good land
use. People knowingly dependent on the land would not willingly see
it cropped or grazed or logged or mined to exhaustion.

I have laid out a vision, and I am skeptical of visions. But this vision
is recommendable at least for its modesty. The scale is small, and I
would be greatly surprised if it should produce even one billionaire. It
is also a practical vision. It exists, no doubt in many versions, because
it is attractive to some of us. But we are going to see it enforced by the
increasingly manifest failures of industrial forms of land use. I don't
think I need to say a lot about these failures beyond just listing them.
The principal ones are these:

1. Erosion and degradation of the soil.
2. Pollution by toxic chemicals, resulting in unswimmable
    streams, inedible fish, and a six-thousand-square-mile "dead
    zone" (one of at least four hundred worldwide) in the Gulf of
    Mexico.
3. Toxic or pathogenic food.
4. Forest ecosystems damaged or destroyed by high-grading,
    clear-cutting, tree monocultures, recreational abuse, deer over-
    population, etc.

5. Land destruction on a gigantic scale by forms of surface mining, culminating in mountaintop removal.
6. Destruction of rural communities and the cultures of husbandry.

For a long time the exorbitant costs and damages of industrial exploitation of land and people were talked about only by a fringe of dissidents and protesters. But now these problems have caught the attention of mainstream reporters and are making their way into public consciousness. To give just one example, *Time* magazine, for August 31, 2009, carried an article on industrial agriculture and industrial food that would have been unimaginable even a year earlier. The article says unconditionally:

> With the exhaustion of the soil, the impact of global warming and the inevitably rising price of oil . . . our industrial style of food production will end sooner or later. . . . Unless Americans radically rethink the way they grow and consume food, they face a future of eroded farmland, hollowed-out countryside, scarier germs, and higher health costs . . .

The good news is that we don't have to be consenting victims of agribusiness-as-usual. To give just one example on the positive side, Wes Jackson and the Land Institute—with the backing of numerous other groups and institutions—have proposed to the Secretary of Agriculture "A 50-Year Farm Bill" that addresses head-on the problems of erosion, toxicity, loss of diversity, and the decline of farm communities. The five-year farm bill—what we have had so far—deals with export policy, consumer issues, subsidies, food stamps, etc., with a bone thrown to ecology by way of never-adequate conservation programs. "A 50-Year Farm Bill," by contrast, comes at agriculture from ecology, and deals directly with issues of land use. The key change proposed by this bill is the increase in the acreage of perennial plants from 20 percent in 2009 to 80 percent in 2059. This change would involve at first increases in pasture and forage crops, and then, starting in 2019, the introduction of perennial grain crops.

The proposed perennialization of agriculture, like the horse and the tractor, would not be a simple choice. It too would be a package deal, and it would go literally to the roots of our problem. The advocates and suppliers of agri-industrial technologies have encouraged us to think of agriculture as an enterprise occurring on top of the ground. We have not been concerned nearly enough with the condition of the soil, with the health and abundance of underground organisms, or with the depth, tenacity, and longevity of the roots of plants. Perhaps we have avoided these subterranean matters because of their darkness and complexity, which belittle our knowledge and our powers of explanation.

The use of perennial plants in agriculture may always levy a tax of humility and require a certain deference to mystery. You may, for example, "manage" your pasture; you may by good management take excellent care of it, keeping it healthy and productive all your life; but you will never know its whole pattern or its whole story, from the long, nutrient-releasing decay of its bedrock, to the cohabitation of its plant species, their foliages and roots, to the teeming communities of the small-to-invisible creatures of sod and topsoil, to the interactions of tame and wild grazers and foragers and their predators, to the birds that live in and above and from it, to the ways in which your work and care affect everything else. No conceivable language or diagram could make it plain. To live with a pasture year after year is certainly to learn more and more, but it is also to learn more and more how small your knowledge is. The predominance of annual monocultures, by contrast, encourages a disastrous pretense of omniscience.

A significant increase in the acreages just of pastures and forages implies—in addition to the obvious result of less soil erosion—a new diversification. Replacing corn and soy beans grown for animal feed with perennial grasses and legumes would reduce erosion and save energy; by extending the seasonal green growth of the fields, it would greatly increase the harvest of solar energy; and it would take cattle, hogs, and poultry out of the animal factories and put them back on farms, back on grass, where they belong. Diversification would tend to reduce the size and increase the number of farms; it would bring more people into agriculture, where at least some of them belong. This is a prospect pleasing to all of us who are devoted to better, kinder ways of using the land. But it involves worries too, and to be as honest as possible I want to speak of a worry.

Most people who understand good land use know that to use our land in the best way, we will need more people on our farms and ranches and in our forests. We need a better ratio of eyes to acres, as Wes Jackson has put it. We need more people skilled in physical work, who have workable minds. How are we going to get them? That is a big worry. They certainly are not going to come ready-made from the "labor pool." And we can hardly expect to get the best work done by underpaying and overworking an underclass of migrant workers— yet another racially denigrated class consigned to "menial" work. I think we will have to go back to our old agrarian ideal, espoused by Thomas Jefferson among many others, of a countryside populated by settled families and stable communities earning a decent liveli- hood from their work and their goods. And let me say emphatically that by "settled families" I mean people of any race or origin who are willing to accept the actual responsibilities and do the actual work that go with the ownership and good use of land. The people who do the land's work should own the land. It should *not* be owned in great monopolistic estates by a class of absentee landlords, as in the latter days of the Roman Empire, and as increasingly now, with us, in the time of our own decadence.

To speak of the need for settled families and stable communities in rural America is to imply at the same time the necessity of extensive and profound cultural change. Good and responsible use of family-sized holdings cannot be expected of people with the dependent and subservient minds of industrial employees. What is required are people independently intelligent and resourceful, skilled in handwork and practical thought, who have forgotten about "professionalism," "official channels," and "overtime."

Now I hope I have said enough to return more pointedly to the problem I started with: our popular and dangerous doctrine of the simple solution. In my lifetime I have witnessed the advent of several solutions that were both large and simple, all ostensibly addressed to one or two problems. The nuclear bomb, the work of "idealistic" scientists, was invented to win a war. It then brought forth "the peaceful atom" to assure military dominance and to solve forever our need for cheap, clean energy. Among other unforeseen results is a string of six industrial sites and waste dumps along the Ohio Valley from Portsmouth to Paducah that will be contaminated, and unimaginably dangerous, virtually forever.

Such simple solutions as nuclear power and, more recently, biofuels have been introduced into contexts, natural or human or both, that its proponents have ignored. Every one, in order to solve a problem or two, which as likely as not it has failed to solve, has caused new problems by which its proponents have been surprised. Every one has been immensely profitable to some, though its real costs, including ecological and social costs, have not been debited against its earnings. We don't have an accurate measure even of the net economic value of any of them.

On September 29, 2009, the *New York Times* reported the latest of a long line of simple solutions in agriculture. This is "a long-awaited breakthrough," namely "a high-technology method to sort the sperm of dairy bulls" so that it "produced 90 percent or more female off-spring, allowing farmers to expand their herds more efficiently."

Well, who in our frantically innovating society is going to quarrel with efficiency? The answer, as usual, is that there will be no quarrel until the desired efficiency crashes into a reality that, as usual, comes as a surprise. In this instance the big surprise was "the economic crisis" that "caused booming dairy exports to dry up and curbed demand at home, sending prices tumbling. At the same time, feed costs remained high …" Overproduction is the inevitable result, which is hardly the right circumstance for the introduction of sorted bull sperm and the consequent increase of the size or productivity of dairy herds.

Here, then, is another example of technological innovation made in ignorance, and therefore in defiance, of context. "Sexed semen" came into use because it made an illusory sort of financial sense: more cows = more milk + booming demand = more money. The presumed efficiency led directly to disaster—for dairy owners but not, I suppose, for the producers of sexed semen—because it did not make economic sense. It failed to make economic sense, we must suppose, because for a long time the dairy industry has failed to make agricultural or ecological sense. Instead of a resilient dairy economy, broadly based upon local demand and diversified small farms capable of adapting quickly to changes of context, we have a gigantic, overfinanced, financially vulnerable dairy industry founded upon the two bubbles of Wall Street delusion and global demand.

The increasingly undeniable failures and dangers of our industrial system of food production are attributable mostly to our cult of simple solutions. The simple-mindedness that produces simple solutions has made us incapable of judging industrial efficiencies and technological breakthroughs within the contexts of actual economy, the disciplines of good land use, or ecological responsibility. Simple solutions will always lead to complex troubles, and simple minds will always be surprised.*

By contrast, the 50-Year Farm Bill—proposing diversification, detoxification, perennialization, and resettlement of our agricultural landscapes—cannot be thought of as simple. It is immediately and obviously complex. It proposes a kind of decency and a kind of justice to ecosystems and the ecosphere, to the communities and cultures of land husbandry, and to human society. It involves much difficulty. It will take a long time. The most we can say in its favor is that it is necessary, for it would solve, not one or two, but many problems. It would bring more people, more hands and eyes, more intelligence, more conscience, more affection into the service of our economic landscapes. If this can happen, it will be a homecoming.

(2009)

---

* On February 19, 2010, an op-ed article in the *New York Times*, by Adam Shriver (a doctoral student in the philosophy-neuroscience-psychology program at Washington University), proposes genetically engineering the brains of animals painfully confined in animal factories so that they cannot feel pain. A practice that is indefensible morally, ecologically, agriculturally, and (if all the costs were accounted) economically, is thus made acceptable if the animals are "engineered" so as not to feel their suffering. The idea that science can be used to shortcut the actual complexity of actual problems has become conventional with some scientists. This dishonors and abuses everything involved, including science.

II

A Nation Rich in Natural Resources

∞

If "economy" means "management of a household," then we have a system of national accounting that bears no resemblance to the national economy whatsoever, for it is not the record of our life at home but the fever chart of our consumption. Our national economy—the health of which might be indicated by our net national product, derived by subtracting our real losses from our real gains—is perhaps a top secret, the existence of which even the government has not yet suspected.

One reason for this is the geographical separation that frequently exists between losses and gains. Agricultural losses occur on the farm and in farming communities, whereas the great gains of agriculture all occur in cities, just as the profits from coal are realized mainly in cities far from where the coal is mined. Almost always the profit is realized by people who are under no pressure or obligation to realize the losses—people, that is, who are so positioned by wealth and power that they need assign no value at all to what is lost. The cost of soil erosion is not deducted from the profit on a packaged beefsteak, just as the loss of forest, topsoil, and human homes on a Kentucky mountainside does not reduce the profit on a ton of coal.

If this peculiar estrangement between losses and gains, between products and their real costs, is institutionalized anywhere, it is in our ubiquitous word, "resource." One definition of this word is close to the meaning of its Latin root, "*resurgere,*" to rise again. In this sense, a resource is a dependable (which is to say a constant) supply; a resource rises again as a spring rises, refilling its basin, after a bucket of water has been dipped out. This is what the topsoil and what the human culture of farming can do under the right "household management," the right economy: They replenish themselves and they can last as long as the earth and the sun. The right economy is right insofar as it respects the source, respects the power of the source to resurge, and does not ask too much.

Another, opposite, definition of resource is "means that can be used to advantage." That, I am afraid, is the definition of the word as we now use it. We look upon everything as a resource, even people; the state of Kentucky, for instance, has a Department of Human Resources. With us, a resource is something that has no value until it has been made into something else. Thus, a tree has value only insofar as it can be made into lumber, and our schools, which are more and more understood and justified as dispensers of "job training," are based on the implicit principle that children have no value until they have been made into employees.

Common sense suggests that it is not possible to make a good thing out of a bad thing. We can see that we cannot prepare a good meal from poor food, produce good food from poor soil, maintain good soil without good farming, or have good farming without a good culture—a culture that places a proper value on the proper maintenance of the natural sources, so that the needed supplies are constantly available. Thus, food is a product both natural and cultural, and good cooking must be said to begin with good farming. A good economy would value our bodily nourishment in *all* of its transformations from the topsoil to the dinner table and beyond, for it would place an appropriate value on our excrement, too, and return it to the soil; in a good economy, there would be no such thing as "waste," bodily or otherwise. At every stage of its making, our nourishment would be a finished product in the sense that at every stage it would be brought to a high order of excellence, but at no stage would it be a finished product in the sense of being done with.

We must also notice that as the natural energy approaches human usability, it passes through a declension of forms less and less complex. A potato is less complex than the topsoil, a steak than a steer, a cooked meal than a farm. If, in the human economy, a squash on the table is worth more than a squash in the field, and a squash in the field is worth more than a bushel of soil, that does not mean that food is more valuable than soil; it means simply that we do not know *how* to value the soil. In its complexity and its potential longevity, the soil exceeds our comprehension; we do not know how to place a just market value on it, and we will never learn how. Its value is inestimable; we must value it, beyond whatever price we put on it, by *respecting* it.

The industrial economy, on the other hand, reduces the value of a thing to its market price, and it sets the market price in accordance with the capacity of a thing to be made into another kind of thing. Thus, a farm is valued *only* for its ability to produce marketable livestock and/or crops; livestock and crops are valued *only* insofar as they can be manufactured into groceries; groceries are valued *only* to the extent that they can be sold to consumers. An absolute division is made at every stage of the industrial process between raw materials, to which, as such, we accord no respect at all, and finished products, which we respect only to the extent of their market value. A lot could be said about the quality of the "finish" of these products, but the critical point here is that, in the industrial economy, value in the form of respect is withheld from the source, and value in the form of price is always determined by reference to a *future* usability—nothing is valued for what it is.

But when nothing is valued for what it is, everything is destined to be wasted. Once the values of things refer only to their future usefulness, then an infinite withdrawal of value from the living present has begun. Nothing (and nobody) can then exist that is not theoretically replaceable by something (or somebody) more valuable. The country that we (or some of us) had thought to make our home becomes instead "a nation rich in natural resources"; the good bounty of the land begins its mechanical metamorphosis into junk, garbage, silt, poison, and other forms of "waste."

The inevitable result of such an economy is that no farm or any other usable property can safely be regarded by anyone as a home, no home is ultimately worthy of our loyalty, nothing is ultimately worth doing, and no place or task or person is worth a lifetime's devotion. "Waste," in such an economy, must eventually include several categories of humans—the unborn, the old, "disinvested" farmers, the unemployed, the "unemployable." Indeed, once our homeland, our source, is regarded as a resource, we are all sliding downward toward the ashheap or the dump.

(1985)

An Argument for Diversity

∞

I live in and have known all my life the northern corner of Henry County, Kentucky. The country here is narrowly creased and folded; it is a varied landscape whose main features are these:

1. A rolling upland of which some of the soil is good and some, because of abuse, is less so. This upland is well suited to mixed farming, which was, in fact, traditional to it, but which is less diversified now than it was a generation ago. Some row-cropping is possible here, but even the best-lying ridges are vulnerable to erosion and probably not more than 10 percent should be broken in any year. It is

a kind of land that needs grass and grazing animals, and it is excellent for this use.

2. Wooded bluffs where the upland breaks over into the valleys of the creeks and the Kentucky River. Along with virtually all of this region, most of these bluffs have been cleared and cropped at one time or another. They should never have been cropped, and because of their extreme vulnerability to erosion they should be logged only with the greatest skill and care. These bluffs are now generally forested, though not many old-growth stands remain.

3. Slopes of gentler declivity below the bluffs and elsewhere. Some of these slopes are grassed and, with close care, are maintainable as pasture. Until World War II they were periodically cropped, in a version of slash-and-burn agriculture that resulted in serious damage by erosion. Now much of this land is covered with trees thirty or forty years old.

4. Finally, there are the creek and river bottoms, some of which are subject to flooding. Much of this land is suitable for intensive row-cropping, which, under the regime of industrial agriculture, has sometimes been too intensive.

Within these four general divisions this country is extremely diverse. To familiarity and experience, the landscape divides into many small facets or aspects differentiated by the kind or quality of soil and by slope, exposure, drainage, rockiness, and so on. In the two centuries during which European races have occupied this part of the country, the best of the land has sometimes been well used, under the influence of good times and good intentions. But virtually none of it has escaped ill use under the influence of bad times or ignorance, need or greed. Some of it—the steeper, more marginal areas—never has been well used. Of virtually all this land it may be said that the national economy has prescribed ways of use but not ways of care. It is now impossible to imagine any immediate way that most of this land might receive excellent care. The economy, as it now is, prescribes plunder of the landowners and abuse of the land.

The connection of the American economy to this place—in comparison, say, to the connection of the American economy to just about any university—has been unregarding and ungenerous. Indeed, the connection has been almost entirely exploitive—and it has never been more exploitive than it is now. Increasingly, from the beginning, most of the money made on the products of this place has been made in other places. Increasingly the ablest young people of this place have gone away to receive a college education, which has given them a "professional status" too often understood as a license to become the predators of such places as this one that they came from. The destruction of the human community, the local economy, and the natural health of such a place as this is now looked upon not as a "trade-off," a possibly regrettable "price of progress," but as a good, virtually a national goal.

Recently I heard, on an early-morning radio program, a university economist explaining the benefits of off-farm work for farm women: that these women are increasingly employed off the farm, she said, has made them "full partners" in the farm's economy. Never mind that this is a symptom of economic desperation and great unhappiness on the farm. And never mind the value, which was more than economic, of these women's previous contribution *on* the farm to the farm family's life and economy—in what was, many of them would have said, a full partnership. *Now* they are "earning 45 percent of total family income"; *now* they are playing "a major role." The 45 percent and the "major role" are allowed to defray all other costs. That the farm family now furnishes labor and (by its increased consumption) income to the economy that is destroying it is seen simply as an improvement. Thus the abstract and extremely tentative value of money is thoughtlessly allowed to replace the particular and fundamental values of the lives of household and community. Obviously, we need to stop thinking about the economic functions of individuals for a while, and try to learn to think of the economic functions of communities and households. We need to try to understand the long-term economies of places—places, that is, that are considered as dwelling places for humans and their fellow creatures, not as exploitable resources.

What happens when farm people take up "off-farm work"? The immediate result is that they must be replaced by chemicals and machines and other purchases from an economy adverse and antipathetic to farming, which means that the remaining farmers are put under yet greater economic pressure to abuse their land. If under the pressure of an adverse economy the soil erodes, soil and water and air are poisoned, the woodlands are wastefully logged, and everything not producing an immediate economic return is neglected, that is apparently understood by most of the society as merely the normal cost of production.

This means, among other things, that the land and its human communities are not being thought about in places of study and leadership, and this failure to think is causing damage. But if one lives in a country place, and if one loves it, one must think about it. Under present circumstances, it is not easy to imagine what might be a proper human economy for the country I have just described. And yet, if one loves it, one must make the attempt; if one loves it, the attempt is irresistible.

Two facts are immediately apparent. One is that the present local economy, based like the economies of most rural places exclusively on the export of raw materials, is ruinous. Another is that the influence of a complex, aggressive national economy upon a simple, passive local economy will also be ruinous. In a varied and versatile countryside, fragile in its composition and extremely susceptible to abuse, requiring close human care and elaborate human skills, able to produce and needing to produce a great variety of products from its soils, what is needed, obviously, is a highly diversified local economy.

We should be producing the fullest variety of foods to be consumed locally, in the countryside itself and in nearby towns and cities: meats, grains, table vegetables, fruits and nuts, dairy products, poultry and eggs. We should be harvesting a sustainable yield of fish from our ponds and streams. Our woodlands, managed for continuous yields, selectively and carefully logged, should be yielding a variety of timber for a variety of purposes: firewood, fence posts, lumber for building, fine woods for furniture makers.

And we should be adding value locally to these local products. What is needed is not the large factory so dear to the hearts of government "developers." To set our whole population to making computers or automobiles would be as gross an error as to use the whole countryside for growing corn or Christmas trees or pulpwood; it would discount everything we have to offer as a community and a place; it would despise our talents and capacities as individuals.

We need, instead, a system of decentralized, small-scale industries to transform the products of our fields and woodlands and streams: small creameries, cheese factories, canneries, grain mills, saw mills, furniture factories, and the like. By "small" I mean simply a size that would not be destructive of the appearance, the health, and the quiet of the countryside. If a factory began to "grow" or to be noisy at night or on Sunday, that would mean that another such factory was needed somewhere else. If waste should occur at any point, that would indicate the need for an enterprise of some other sort. If poison or pollution resulted from any enterprise, that would be understood as an indication that something was absolutely wrong, and a correction would be made. Small scale, of course, makes such changes and corrections more thinkable and more possible than does large scale.

I realize that, by now, my argument has crossed a boundary line of which everyone in our "realistic" society is keenly aware. I will be perceived to have crossed over into "utopianism" or fantasy. Unless I take measures to prevent it, I am going to hear somebody say, "All that would be very nice, if it were possible. Can't you be realistic?"

Well, let me take measures to prevent it. I am not, I admit, optimistic about the success of this kind of thought. Otherwise, my intention, above all, is to be realistic; I wish to be practical. The question here is simply that of convention. Do I want to be realistic according to the conventions of the industrial economy and the military state, or according to what I know of reality? To me, an economy that sees the life of a community or a place as expendable, and reckons its value only in terms of money, is not acceptable because it is *not* realistic. I am thinking as I believe we must think if we wish to discuss the *best* uses of people, places, and things, and if we wish to give affection some standing in our thoughts.

If we wish to make the best use of people, places, and things, then we are going to have to deal with a law that reads about like this: As the quality of use increases, the scale of use (that is, the size of operations) will decline, the tools will become simpler, and the methods and the skills will become more complex. That is a difficult law for us to believe, because we have assumed otherwise for a long time, and yet our experience overwhelmingly suggests that it *is* a law, and that the penalties for disobeying it are severe.

I am making a plea for diversity not only because diversity exists and is pleasant, but also because it is necessary and we need more of it. For an example, let me return to the countryside I described at the beginning of this essay. From birth, I have been familiar with this place and have heard it talked about and thought about. For the last twenty-five years I have been increasingly involved in the use and improvement of a little part of it. As a result of some failures and some successes, I have learned some things about it. I am certain, however, that I do not know the best way to use this land. Nor do I believe that anyone else does. I no longer expect to live to see it come to its best use. But I am beginning to see what is needed, and everywhere the need is for diversity. This is the need of every American rural land-scape that I am acquainted with. We need a greater range of species and varieties of plants and animals, of human skills and methods, so that the use may be fitted ever more sensitively and elegantly to the place. Our places, in short, are asking us questions, some of them urgent questions, and we do not have the answers.

The answers, if they are to come and if they are to work, must be developed in the presence of the user and the land; they must be developed to some degree *by* the user *on* the land. The present practice of handing down from on high policies and technologies developed without consideration of the nature and the needs of the land and the people has not worked, and it cannot work. Good agriculture and forestry cannot be "invented" by self-styled smart people in the offices and laboratories of a centralized economy and then sold at the highest possible profit to the supposedly dumb country people. That is not the way good land use comes about. And it does not matter how the methodologies so developed and handed down are labeled; whether "industrial" or "conventional" or "organic" or "sustainable," the professional or professorial condescension that is blind to the primacy of the union between individual people and individual places is ruinous. The challenge to the would-be scientists of an ecologically sane agriculture, as David Ehrenfeld has written, is "to provide unique and particular answers to questions about a farmer's unique and particular land." The proper goal, he adds, is *not* merely to "substitute the cult of the benevolent ecologist for the cult of the benevolent sales representative."

The question of what a beloved country is to be used for quickly becomes inseparable from the questions of who is to use it or who is to prescribe its uses, and what will be the ways of using it. If we speak simply of the use of "a country," then only the first question is asked, and it is asked only by its would-be users. It is not until we speak of "a beloved country"—a particular country, particularly loved—that the question about ways of use will arise. It arises because, loving our country, we see where we are, and we see that present ways of use are not adequate. They are not adequate because such local cultures and economies as we once had have been stunted or destroyed. As a nation, we have attempted to substitute the *concepts* of "land use," "agribusiness," "development," and the like for the *culture* of stewardship and husbandry. And this change is not a result merely of economic pressures and adverse social values; it comes also from the state of affairs in our educational system, especially in our universities.

It is readily evident, once affection is allowed into the discussion of "land use," that the life of the mind, as presently constituted in the universities, is of no help. The sciences are of no help, indeed are destructive, because they work, by principle, outside the demands, checks, and corrections of affection. The problem with this "scientific objectivity" becomes immediately clear when science undertakes to "apply" itself to land use. The problem simply is that land users are using people, places, and things that cannot be well used without affection. To be well used, creatures and places must be used sympathetically, just as they must be known sympathetically to be well known. The economist to whom it is of no concern whether or not a family loves its farm will almost inevitably aid and abet the destruction of family farming. The "animal scientist" to whom it is of no concern whether or not animals suffer will almost inevitably aid and abet the destruction of the decent old ideal of animal husbandry and, as a consequence, increase the suffering of animals. I hope that my country may be delivered from the remote, cold abstractions of university science.

But "the humanities," as presently constituted in the universities, are of no help either, and indeed, with respect to the use of a beloved country, they too have been destructive. (The closer I have come to using the term "humanities," the less satisfactory it has seemed to me; by it I mean everything that is not a "science," another unsatisfactory term.) The humanities have been destructive not because they have been misapplied, but because they have been so frequently understood by their academic stewards as not applicable. The scientific ideals of objectivity and specialization have now crept into the humanities and made themselves at home. This has happened, I think, because the humanities have come to be infected with a suspicion of their uselessness or worthlessness in the face of the provability or workability or profitability of the applied sciences. The conviction is now widespread, for instance, that "a work of art" has no purpose but to be itself. Or if it is allowed that a poem, for instance, has a meaning, then it is a meaning peculiar to its author, its time, or its convention. A poem, in short, is a relic as soon as it is composed; it can be taught, but it cannot teach. The issue of its truth and pertinence is not raised because literary study is conducted with about the same anxiety for "control" as is scientific study. The context of a poem is its text, or the context of its history and criticism as a text. I have not, of course, read all the books or sat in all the classrooms, but my impression is that not much importance is attached to the question of the truth of poems. My impression is that *Comus*, for example, is not often taught as an argument with a history and a sequel, with the gravest importance for us in our dilemma now. My impression is that the great works are taught less and less as Ananda Coomaraswamy said they should be: with the recognition "that nothing will have been accomplished unless men's lives are affected and their values changed by what we have to show." My impression is that in the humanities as in the sciences the world is increasingly disallowed as a context. I hope that my country may be delivered from the objectivity of the humanities.

Without a beloved country as context, the arts and the sciences become oriented to the careers of their practitioners, and the intellectual life to intellectual (and bureaucratic) procedures. And so in the universities we see forming an intellectual elite more and more exclusively accomplished in procedures such as promotion, technological innovation, publication, and grant-getting. The context of a beloved country, moreover, implies an academic standard that is not inflatable or deflatable. The standard—the physical, intellectual, political, ecological, economic, and spiritual health of the country—cannot be too high; it will be as high, simply, as we have the love, the vision, and the courage to make it.

I would like my country to be seen and known with an attentiveness that is schooled and skilled. I would like it to be loved with a minutely particular affection and loyalty. I would like the work in it to be practical and loving and respectful and forbearing. In order for these things to happen, the sciences and the humanities are going to have to come together again in the presence of the practical problems of individual places, and of local knowledge and local love in individual people— people able to see, know, think, feel, and act coherently and well without the modern instinct of deference to the "outside expert."

What should the sciences have to say to a citizen in search of the criteria by which to determine the best use of a beloved place or countryside, or of the technical or moral means by which to limit that use to its best use? What should the humanities have to say to a scientist—or, for that matter, a citizen—in search of the cultural instructions that might effectively govern the use of a beloved place? These questions or such questions could reunite the sciences and the humanities. That a scientist and an artist can speak and work together in response to such questions I know from my own experience. All that is necessary is a mutuality of concern and a mutual willingness to speak common English. When friends speak across these divisions or out of their "departments," in mutual concern for a beloved country, then it is clear that these diverse disciplines are not "competing interests," as the university structure and academic folklore suggest, but interests with legitimate claims on all minds. It is only when the country becomes an abstraction, a prize of conquest, that these interests compete—though, of course, when that has happened *all* interests compete.

But in order to assure that a beloved country might be lovingly used, the sciences and the humanities will have to do more than mend their divorce at "the university level"; they will also have to mend their divorce from the common culture, by which I do not mean the "popular culture," but rather the low and local wisdom that is now either relegated to the compartments of anthropology or folklore or "oral history," or not attended to at all.

Some time ago, after I had given a lecture at a college in Ohio, a gentleman came up and introduced himself to me as a fellow Kentuckian.

"Where in Kentucky are you from?" I asked.

"Oh, a little place you probably never heard of—North Middletown."

"I *have* heard of North Middletown," I said. "It was the home of my father's great friend John W. Jones."

"Well, John W. Jones was my uncle."

I told him then of my father's and my own respect for Mr. Jones.

"I want to tell you a story about Uncle John," he said. And he told me this:

When his Uncle John was president of the bank in North Middletown, his policy was to give a loan to any graduate of the North Middletown high school who wanted to go to college and needed the money. This practice caused great consternation to the bank examiners who came and found those unsecured loans on the books and no justification for them except Mr. Jones' conviction that it was right to make them.

As it turned out, it was right in more than principle, for in the many years that Mr. Jones was president of the bank, making those "unsound loans," *all* of the loans were repaid; he never lost a dime on a one of them.

I do not mean to raise here the question of the invariable goodness of a college education, which I doubt. My point in telling this story is that Mr. Jones was acting from a kind of knowledge, inestimably valuable and probably indispensable, that comes out of common culture and that cannot be taught as a part of the formal curriculum of a school. The students whose education he enabled were not taught this knowledge at the colleges they attended. What he knew—and this involved his knowledge of himself, his tradition, his community, and everybody in it—was that trust, in the circumstances then present, could beget trustworthiness. This is the kind of knowledge, obviously, that is fundamental to the possibility of community life and to certain good possibilities in the characters of people. Though I don't believe that it can be taught and learned in a university, I think that it should be known about and respected in a university, and I don't know where, in the sciences and the humanities as presently constituted, students would be led to suspect, much less to honor, its existence. It is certainly no part of banking or of economics as now taught and practiced. It is a part of community life, which most scientists ignore in their professional pursuits, and which most people in the humanities seem to regard as belonging to a past now useless or lost or dispensed with.

Let me give another, more fundamental example. My brother, who is a lawyer, recently had as a client an elderly man named Bennie Yeary who had farmed for many years a farm of about three hundred acres of hilly and partly forested land. His farm and the road to his house had been damaged by a power company.

Seeking to determine the value of the land, my brother asked him if he had ever logged his woodlands. Mr. Yeary answered, "Yes, sir, since 1944 . . . I have never robbed [the land]. I have always just cut a little out where I thought it needed it. I have got as much timber right now, I am satisfied . . . as I had when I started mill runs here in '44."

That we should not rob the land is a principle to be found readily enough in the literary culture. That it came into literature out of the common culture is suggested by the fact that it is commonly phrased in this way by people who have not inherited the literary culture. That we should not rob the land, anyhow, is a principle that can be learned from books. But the ways of living on the land so as not to rob it probably

cannot be learned from books, and this is made clear by a further
exchange between my brother and Mr. Yeary.

They came to the question of what was involved in the damage
to the road, and the old farmer said that the power company had
destroyed thirteen or fourteen water breaks. A water break is a low
mound of rock and earth built to divert the water out of a hilly road.
It is a means of preventing erosion both of the roadbed and of the
land alongside it, one of the ways of living on the land without rob-
bing it.

"How long ... had it been since you had those water breaks con-
structed in there?"

"I had been working on them ... off and on, for about twelve years,
putting them water breaks in. I hauled rocks out of my fields ... and
I would dig out, bury these rocks down, and take the sledgehammer
and beat rock in here and make this water break."

The way to make a farm road that will not rob the land cannot be
learned from books, then, because the long use of such a road is a part
of the proper way of making it, and because the use and improvement
of the road are intimately involved with the use and improvement of
the place. It is of the utmost importance that the rocks to make the
water breaks were hauled from the fields. Mr. Yeary's solution did not,
like the typical industrial solution, involve the making of a problem,
or a series of problems, elsewhere. It involved the making of a solution
elsewhere: The same work that improved the road improved the fields.
Such work requires not only correct principles, skill, and industry,
but a knowledge of local particulars and many years; it involves slow,
small adjustments in response to questions asked by a particular place.
And this is true in general of the patterns and structures of a proper
human use of a beloved country, as examination of the traditional
landscapes of the Old World will readily show: They were made by
use as much as by skill.

This implication of use in the making of essential artifacts and the maintenance of the landscape—which are to so large an extent the making and the maintenance of culture—brings us to the inescapable final step in an argument for diversity: the realization that without a diversity of people we cannot maintain a diversity of anything else. By a diversity of people I do not mean a diversity of specialists, but a diversity of people elegantly suited to live in their places and to bring them to their best use, whether the use is that of uselessness, as in a place left wild, or that of the highest sustainable productivity. The most abundant diversity of creatures and ways cannot be maintained in preserves, zoos, museums, and the like, but only in the occupations and the pleasures of an appropriately diversified human economy.

The proper ways of using a beloved country are "humanities," I think, and are as complex, difficult, interesting, and worthy as any of the rest. But they defy the present intellectual and academic categories. They are *both* science and art, knowing and doing. Indispensable as these ways are to the success of human life, they have no place and no standing in the present structures of our intellectual life. The purpose, indeed, of the present structures of our intellectual life has been to educate them out of existence. I think I know where in any university my brother's client, Mr. Yeary, would be laughed at or ignored or tape-recorded or classified. I don't know where he would be appropriately honored. The scientific disciplines certainly do not honor him, and the "humane" ones almost as certainly do not. We would have to go some distance back in the literary tradition—back to Thomas Hardy at least, and before Hardy to Wordsworth—to find the due respect paid to such a person. He *has* been educated almost out of existence, and yet an understanding of his importance and worth would renew the life of the mind in this country, in the university and out.

(1988)

Economy and Pleasure

∞

To those who still uphold the traditions of religious and political thought that influenced the shaping of our society and the founding of our government, it is astonishing, and of course discouraging, to see economics now elevated to the position of ultimate justifier and explainer of all the affairs of our daily life, and competition enshrined as the sovereign principle and ideal of economics.

As thousands of small farms and small local businesses of all kinds falter and fail under the effects of adverse economic policies or live under the threat of what we complacently call "scientific progress," the economist sits in the calm of professorial tenure and government subsidy, commenting and explaining for the illumination of the press and the general public. If those who fail happen to be fellow humans, neighbors, children of God, and citizens of the republic, all that is outside the purview of the economist. As the farmers go under, as communities lose their economic supports, as all of rural America sits as if condemned in the shadow of the "free market" and "revolutionary science," the economist announces pontifically to the press that "there will be some winners and some losers"—as if that might justify and clarify everything, or anything. The sciences, one gathers, mindlessly serve economics, and the humanities defer abjectly to the sciences. All assume, apparently, that we are in the grip of the determination of economic laws that are the laws of the universe. The newspapers quote the economists as the ultimate authorities. We read their pronouncements, knowing that the last word has been said.

"Science," President Reagan says, "tells us that the breakthroughs in superconductivity bring us to the threshold of a new age." He is speaking to "a federal conference on the commercial applications of the new technology," and we know that by "science" he means scientists in the pay of corporations. "It is our task at this conference," he says, "to herald in that new age with a rush." A part of his program to accomplish this task is a proposal to "relax" the antitrust laws.[1] Thus even the national executive and our legal system itself must now defer to the demands of "the economy." Whatever "new age" is at hand at the moment must be heralded in "with a rush" because of the profits available to those who will rush it in.

It seems that we have been reduced almost to a state of absolute economics, in which people and all other creatures and things may be considered purely as economic "units," or integers of production, and in which a human being may be dealt with, as John Ruskin put it, "merely as a covetous machine."[2] And the voices bitterest to hear are those saying that all this destructive work of mindless genius, money, and power is regrettable but cannot be helped.

Perhaps it cannot. Surely we would be fools if, having understood the logic of this terrible process, we assumed that it might not go on in its glutton's optimism until it achieves the catastrophe that is its logical end. But let us suppose that a remedy is possible. If so, perhaps the best beginning would be in understanding the falseness and silliness of the economic ideal of competition, which is destructive both of nature and of human nature because it is untrue to both.

The ideal of competition always implies, and in fact requires, that any community must be divided into a class of winners and a class of losers. This division is radically different from other social divisions: that of the more able and the less able, or that of the richer and the poorer, or even that of the rulers and the ruled. These latter divisions have existed throughout history and at times, at least, have been ameliorated by social and religious ideals that instructed the strong to help the weak. As a purely economic ideal, competition does not contain or imply any such instructions. In fact, the defenders of the ideal of competition have never known what to do with or for the losers. The losers simply accumulate in human dumps, like stores of industrial waste, until they gain enough misery and strength to overpower the winners. The idea that the displaced and dispossessed "should seek retraining and get into another line of work" is, of course, utterly cynical; it is only the hand-washing practiced by officials and experts.[3] A loser, by definition, is somebody whom nobody knows what to do with. There is no limit to the damage and the suffering implicit in this willingness that losers should exist as a normal economic cost.

The danger of the ideal of competition is that it neither proposes nor implies any limits. It proposes simply to lower costs at any cost, and to raise profits at any cost. It does not hesitate at the destruction of the life of a family or the life of a community. It pits neighbor against neighbor as readily as it pits buyer against seller. Every transaction is *meant* to involve a winner and a loser. And for this reason the human economy is pitted without limit against nature. For in the unlimited competition of neighbor and neighbor, buyer and seller, all available means must be used; none may be spared.

I will be told that indeed there are limits to economic competitiveness as now practiced—that, for instance, one is not allowed to kill one's competitor. But, leaving aside the issue of whether or not murder would be acceptable as an economic means if the stakes were high enough, it is a fact that the destruction of life is a part of the daily business of economic competition as now practiced. If one person is willing to take another's property or to accept another's ruin as a normal result of economic enterprise, then he is willing to destroy that other person's life as it is and as it desires to be. That this person's biological existence has been spared seems merely incidental; it was spared because it was not worth anything. That this person is now "free" to "seek retraining and get into another line of work" signifies only that his life as it was has been destroyed.

But there is another implication in the limitlessness of the ideal of competition that is politically even more ominous: namely, that unlimited economic competitiveness proposes an unlimited concentration of economic power. Economic anarchy, like any other free-for-all, tends inevitably toward dominance by the strongest. If it is normal for economic activity to divide the community into a class of winners and a class of losers, then the inescapable implication is that the class of winners will become ever smaller, the class of losers ever larger. And that, obviously, is now happening: The usable property of our country, once divided somewhat democratically, is owned by fewer and fewer people every year. That the president of the republic can, without fear, propose the "relaxation" of antitrust laws in order to "rush" the advent of a commercial "new age" suggests not merely that we are "rushing" toward plutocracy, but that this is now a permissible goal for the would-be winning class for which Mr. Reagan speaks and acts, and a burden acceptable to nearly everybody else.

Nowhere, I believe, has this grossly oversimplified version of economics made itself more at home than in the land-grant universities. The colleges of agriculture, for example, having presided over the now nearly completed destruction of their constituency—the farm people and the farm communities—are now scrambling to ally themselves more firmly than ever, not with "the rural home and rural life"[4] that were, and are, their trust, but with the technocratic aims and corporate interests that are destroying the rural home and rural life. This, of course, is only a new intensification of an old alliance. The revolution that began with machines and chemicals proposes now to continue with automation, computers, and biotechnology. That this has been and is a revolution is undeniable. It has not been merely a "scientific revolution," as its proponents sometimes like to call it, but also an economic one, involving great and profound changes in property ownership and the distribution of real wealth. It has done by insidious tendency what the communist revolutions have done by fiat: It has dispossessed the people and usurped the power and integrity of community life.

This work has been done, and is still being done, under the heading of altruism: Its aims, as its proponents never tire of repeating, are to "serve agriculture" and to "feed the world." These aims, as stated, are irreproachable; as pursued, they raise a number of doubts. Agriculture, it turns out, is to be served strictly according to the rules of competitive economics. The aim is "to make farmers more competitive" and "to make American agriculture more competitive." Against whom, we must ask, are our farmers and our agriculture to be made more competitive? And we must answer, because we know: Against other farmers, at home and abroad. Now, if the colleges of agriculture "serve agriculture" by helping farmers to compete against one another, what do they propose to do to help the farmers who have been outcompeted? Well, those people are not farmers anymore, and therefore are of no concern to the academic servants of agriculture. Besides, they are the beneficiaries of the inestimable liberty to "seek retraining and get into another line of work."

And so the colleges of agriculture, entrusted though they are to serve the rural home and rural life, give themselves over to a hysterical rhetoric of "change," "the future," "the frontiers of modern science," "competition," "the competitive edge," "the cutting edge," "early adoption," and the like, as if there is nothing worth learning from the past and nothing worth preserving in the present. The idea of the teacher and scholar as one called upon to preserve and pass on a common cultural and natural birthright has been almost entirely replaced by the idea of the teacher and scholar as a developer of "human capital" and a bestower of economic advantage. The ambition is to make the university an "economic resource" in a competition for wealth and power that is local, national, and global. Of course, all this works directly against the rural home and rural life, because it works directly against community.

There is no denying that competitiveness is a part of the life both of an individual and of a community, or that, within limits, it is a useful and necessary part. But it is equally obvious that no individual can lead a good or a satisfying life under the rule of competition, and that no community can succeed except by limiting somehow the competitiveness of its members. One cannot maintain one's "competitive edge" if one helps other people. The advantage of "early adoption" would disappear—it would not be thought of—in a community that put a proper value on mutual help. Such advantages would not be thought of by people intent on loving their neighbors as themselves. And it is impossible to imagine that there can be any reconciliation between local and national competitiveness and global altruism. The ambition to "feed the world" or "feed the hungry," rising as it does out of the death struggle of farmer with farmer, proposes not the filling of stomachs, but the engorgement of "the bottom line." The strangest of all the doctrines of the cult of competition, in which admittedly there must be losers as well as winners, is that the result of competition is inevitably good for everybody, that altruistic ends may be met by a system without altruistic motives or altruistic means.

In agriculture, competitiveness has been based throughout the industrial era on constantly accelerating technological change—the very *principle* of agricultural competitiveness is ever-accelerating change—and this has encouraged an ever-accelerating dependency on purchased products, products purchased ever farther from home. Community, however, aspires toward stability. It strives to balance change with constancy. That is why community life places such high value on neighborly love, marital fidelity, local loyalty, the integrity and continuity of family life, respect for the old, and instruction of the young. And a vital community draws its life, so far as possible, from local sources. It prefers to solve its problems, for example, by nonmonetary exchanges of help, not by buying things. A community cannot survive under the rule of competition.

But the land-grant universities, in espousing the economic determinism of the industrialists, have caught themselves in a logical absurdity that they may finally discover to be dangerous to themselves. If competitiveness is the economic norm, and the "competitive edge" the only recognized social goal, then how can these institutions justify public support? Why, in other words, should the public be willing to permit a corporation to profit privately from research that has been subsidized publicly? Why should not the industries be required to afford their own research, and why should not the laws of competition and the free market—if indeed they perform as advertised—enable industries to do their own research a great deal more cheaply than the universities can do it?

The question that we finally come to is a practical one, though it is not one that is entirely answerable by empirical methods: Can a university, or a nation, *afford* this exclusive rule of competition, this purely economic economy? The great fault of this approach to things is that it is so drastically reductive; it does not permit us to live and work as human beings, as the best of our inheritance defines us. Rats and roaches live by competition under the law of supply and demand; it is the privilege of human beings to live under the laws of justice and mercy. It is impossible not to notice how little the proponents of the ideal of competition have to say about honesty, which is the fundamental economic virtue, and how *very* little they have to say about community, compassion, and mutual help.

But what the ideal of competition most flagrantly and disastrously excludes is affection. The affections, John Ruskin said, are "an anomalous force, rendering every one of the ordinary political economist's calculations nugatory; while, even if he desired to introduce this new element into his estimates, he has no power of dealing with it; for the affections only become a true motive power when they ignore every other motive power and condition of political economy." [5] Thus, if we are sane, we do not dismiss or abandon our infant children or our aged parents because they are too young or too old to work. For human beings, affection is the ultimate motive, because the force that powers us, as Ruskin also said, is not "steam, magnetism, or gravitation," but "a Soul."

I would like now to attempt to talk about economy from the standpoint of affection—or, as I am going to call it, pleasure, advancing just a little beyond Ruskin's term, for pleasure is, so to speak, affection in action. There are obvious risks in approaching an economic problem by a way that is frankly emotional—to talk, for example, about the pleasures of nature and the pleasures of work. But these risks seem to me worth taking, for what I am trying to deal with here is the grief that we increasingly suffer as a result of the loss of those pleasures.

It is necessary, at the outset, to make a distinction between pleasure that is true or legitimate and pleasure that is not. We know that a pleasure can be as heavily debited as an economy. Some people undoubtedly thought it pleasant, for example, to have the most onerous tasks of their economy performed by black slaves. But this proved to be a pleasure that was temporary and dangerous. It lived by an enormous indebtedness that was inescapably to be paid not in money, but in misery, waste, and death. The pleasures of fossil fuel combustion and nuclear "security" are, as we are beginning to see, similarly debited to the future. These pleasures are in every way analogous to the self-indulgent pleasures of individuals. They are pleasures that we are allowed to have merely to the extent that we can ignore or defer the logical consequences.

That there is pleasure in competition is not to be doubted. We know from childhood that winning is fun. But we probably begin to grow up when we begin to sympathize with the loser—that is, when we begin to understand that competition involves costs as well as benefits. Sometimes perhaps, as in the most innocent games, the benefits are all to the winner and the costs all to the loser. But when the competition is more serious, when the stakes are higher and greater power is used, then we know that the winner shares in the cost, sometimes disastrously. In war, for example, even the winner is a loser. And this is equally true of our present economy: In unlimited economic competition, the winners are losers; that they may appear to be winners is owing only to their temporary ability to charge their costs to other people or to nature.

But a victory over community or nature can be won only at everybody's cost. For example, we now have in the United States many landscapes that have been defeated—temporarily or permanently—by strip mining, by clear-cutting, by poisoning, by bad farming, or by various styles of "development" that have subjugated their sites entirely to human purposes. These landscapes have been defeated for the benefit of what are assumed to be victorious landscapes: the suburban housing developments and the places of amusement (the park systems, the recreational wildernesses) of the winners—so far—in the economy. But these victorious landscapes and their human inhabitants are already paying the costs of their defeat of other landscapes: in air and water pollution, overcrowding, inflated prices, and various diseases of body and mind. Eventually, the cost will be paid in scarcity or want of necessary goods.

Is it possible to look beyond this all-consuming "rush" of winning and losing to the possibility of countrysides, a nation of countrysides, in which use is not synonymous with defeat? It is. But in order to do so we must consider our pleasures. Since we all know, from our own and our nation's experience, of some pleasures that are canceled by their costs, and of some that result in unredeemable losses and miseries, it is natural to wonder if there may not be such phenomena as *net* pleasures, pleasures that are free or without a permanent cost. And we know that there are. These are the pleasures that we take in our own lives, our own wakefulness in this world, and in the company of other people and other creatures—pleasures innate in the Creation and in our own good work. It is in these pleasures that we possess the likeness to God that is spoken of in Genesis.

"This curious world we inhabit is more wonderful than convenient; more beautiful than it is useful; it is more to be admired and enjoyed than used." [6] Henry David Thoreau said that to his graduating class at Harvard in 1837. We may assume that to most of them it sounded odd, as to most of the Harvard graduating class of 1987 it undoubtedly still would. But perhaps we will be encouraged to take him seriously, if we recognize that this idea is not something that Thoreau made up out of thin air. When he uttered it, he may very well have been remembering Revelation 4:11: "Thou art worthy, O Lord, to receive glory and honour and power: for thou hast created all things, and for thy pleasure they are and were created." That God created "all things" is in itself an uncomfortable thought, for in our workaday world we can hardly avoid preferring some things above others, and this makes it hard to imagine *not* doing so. That God created all things for His pleasure, and that they continue to exist because they please Him, is formidable doctrine indeed, as far as possible both from the "anthropocentric" utilitarianism that some environmentalist critics claim to find in the Bible and from the grouchy spirituality of many Christians.

It would be foolish, probably, to suggest that God's pleasure in all things can be fully understood or appreciated by mere humans. The passage suggests, however, that our truest and profoundest religious experience may be the simple, unasking pleasure in the existence of other creatures that *is* possible to humans. It suggests that God's pleasure in all things must be respected by us in our use of things, and even in our displeasure in some things. It suggests too that we have an obligation to preserve God's pleasure in all things, and surely this means not only that we must not misuse or abuse anything, but also that there must be some things and some places that by common agreement we do not use at all, but leave wild. This bountiful and lovely thought that all creatures are pleasing to God—and potentially pleasing, therefore, to us—is unthinkable from the point of view of an economy divorced from pleasure, such as the one we have now, which completely discounts the capacity of people to be affectionate toward what they do and what they use and where they live and the other people and creatures with whom they live.

It may be argued that our whole society is more devoted to plea-sure than any whole society ever was in the past, that we support in fact a great variety of pleasure industries and that these are thriving as never before. But that would seem only to prove my point. That there can be pleasure industries at all, exploiting our apparently limitless inability to be pleased, can only mean that our economy is divorced from pleasure and that pleasure is gone from our workplaces and our dwelling places. Our workplaces are more and more exclusively given over to production, and our dwelling places to consumption. And this accounts for the accelerating division of our country into defeated landscapes and victorious (but threatened) landscapes.

More and more, we take for granted that work must be destitute of pleasure. More and more, we assume that if we want to be pleased we must wait until evening, or the weekend, or vacation, or retire-ment. More and more, our farms and forests resemble our factories and offices, which in turn more and more resemble prisons—why else should we be so eager to escape them? We recognize defeated landscapes by the absence of pleasure from them. We are defeated at work because our work gives us no pleasure. We are defeated at home because we have no pleasant work there. We turn to the pleasure industries for relief from our defeat, and are again defeated, for the pleasure industries can thrive and grow only upon our dissatisfaction with them.

Where is our comfort but in the free, uninvolved, finally mysterious beauty and grace of this world that we did not make, that has no price? Where is our sanity but there? Where is our pleasure but in working and resting kindly in the presence of this world?

And in the right sort of economy, our pleasure would not be merely an addition or by-product or reward; it would be both an empowerment of our work and its indispensable measure. Pleasure, Ananda Coomaraswamy said, *perfects* work. In order to have leisure and pleasure, we have mechanized and automated and computerized our work. But what does this do but divide us ever more from our work and our products—and, in the process, from one another and the world? What have farmers done when they have mechanized and computerized their farms? They have removed themselves and their pleasure from their work.

I was fortunate, late in his life, to know Henry Besuden of Clark County, Kentucky, the premier Southdown sheep breeder and one of the great farmers of his time. He told me once that his first morning duty in the spring and early summer was to saddle his horse and ride across his pastures to see the condition of the grass when it was freshest from the moisture and coolness of the night. What he wanted to see in his pastures at that time of year, when his spring lambs would be fattening, was what he called "bloom"—by which he meant not flowers, but a certain visible delectability. He recognized it, of course, by his delight in it. He was one of the best of the traditional livestockmen—the husbander or husband of his animals.

As such, he was not interested in "statistical indicators" of his flock's "productivity." He wanted his sheep to be pleased. If they were pleased with their pasture, they would eat eagerly, drink well, rest, and grow. He knew their pleasure by his own.

The nearly intolerable irony in our dissatisfaction is that we have removed pleasure from our work in order to remove "drudgery" from our lives. If I could pick any rule of industrial economics to receive a thorough reexamination by our people, it would be the one that says that all hard physical work is "drudgery" and not worth doing. There are of course many questions surrounding this issue: What is the work? In whose interest is it done? Where and in what circumstances is it done? How well and to what result is it done? In whose company is it done? How long does it last? And so forth. But this issue is personal and so needs to be reexamined by everybody. The argument, if it is that, can proceed only by personal testimony.

I can say, for example, that the tobacco harvest in my own home country involves the hardest work that I have done in any quantity. In most of the years of my life, from early boyhood until now, I have taken part in the tobacco cutting. This work usually occurs at some time between the last part of August and the first part of October. Usually the weather is hot; usually we are in a hurry. The work is extremely demanding, and often, because of the weather, it has the character of an emergency. Because all of the work still must be done by hand, this event has maintained much of its old character; it is very much the sort of thing the agriculture experts have had in mind when they have talked about freeing people from drudgery.

That the tobacco cutting *can* be drudgery is obvious. If there is too much of it, if it goes on too long, if one has no interest in it, if one cannot reconcile oneself to the misery involved in it, if one does not like or enjoy the company of one's fellow workers, then drudgery would be the proper name for it.

But for me, and I think for most of the men and women who have been my companions in this work, it has not been drudgery. None of us would say that we take pleasure in all of it all of the time, but we do take pleasure in it, and sometimes the pleasure can be intense and clear. Many of my dearest memories come from these times of hardest work.

The tobacco cutting is the most protracted social occasion of our year. Neighbors work together; they are together all day every day for weeks. The quiet of the work is not much interrupted by machine noises, and so there is much talk. There is the talk involved in the management of the work. There is incessant speculation about the weather. There is much laughter; because of the unrelenting difficulty of the work, everything funny or amusing is relished. And there are memories.

The crew to which I belong is the product of kinships and friendships going far back; my own earliest associations with it occurred nearly forty years ago. And so as we work we have before us not only the present crop and the present fields, but other crops and other fields that are remembered. The tobacco cutting is a sort of ritual of remembrance. Old stories are retold; the dead and the absent are remembered. Some of the best talk I have ever listened to I have heard during these times, and I am especially moved to think of the care that is sometimes taken to speak well—that is, to speak fittingly—of the dead and the absent. The conversation, one feels, is ancient. Such talk in barns and at row ends must go back without interruption to the first farmers. How long it may continue is now an uneasy question; not much longer perhaps, but we do not know. We only know that while it lasts it can carry us deeply into our shared life and the happiness of farming.

On many days we have had somebody's child or somebody's children with us, playing in the barn or around the patch while we worked, and these have been our best days. One of the most regrettable things about the industrialization of work is the segregation of children. As industrial work excludes the dead by social mobility and technological change, it excludes children by haste and danger. The small scale and the handwork of our tobacco cutting permit margins both temporal and spatial that accommodate the play of children. The children play at the grownups' work, as well as at their own play. In their play the children learn to work; they learn to know their elders and their country. And the presence of playing children means invariably that the grownups play too from time to time.

(I am perforce aware of the problems and the controversies about tobacco. I have spoken of the tobacco harvest here simply because it is the only remaining farm job in my part of the country that still involves a traditional neighborliness.)

Ultimately, in the argument about work and how it should be done, one has only one's pleasure to offer. It is possible, as I have learned again and again, to be in one's place, in such company, wild or domestic, and with such pleasure, that one cannot think of another place that one would prefer to be—or of another place at all. One does not miss or regret the past, or fear or long for the future. Being there is simply all, and is enough. Such times give one the chief standard and the chief reason for one's work.

Last December, when my granddaughter, Katie, had just turned five, she stayed with me one day while the rest of the family was away from home. In the afternoon we hitched a team of horses to the wagon and hauled a load of dirt for the barn floor. It was a cold day, but the sun was shining; we hauled our load of dirt over the tree-lined gravel lane beside the creek—a way well known to her mother and to my mother when they were children. As we went along, Katie drove the team for the first time in her life. She did very well, and she was proud of herself. She said that her mother would be proud of her, and I said that I was proud of her.

We completed our trip to the barn, unloaded our load of dirt, smoothed it over the barn floor, and wetted it down. By the time we started back up the creek road the sun had gone over the hill and the air had turned bitter. Katie sat close to me in the wagon, and we did not say anything for a long time. I did not say anything because I was afraid that Katie was not saying anything because she was cold and tired and miserable and perhaps homesick; it was impossible to hurry much, and I was unsure how I would comfort her.

But then, after a while, she said, "Wendell, isn't it fun?"

(1988)

NOTES
1 "Reagan calls for effort to find commercial uses for superconductors," *Louisville Courier-Journal*, July 29, 1987, p. A3.
2 John Ruskin, *Unto This Last* (Lincoln: University of Nebraska Press, 1967), p. 11.
3 Reed Karaim, "Loss of million farms in 14 years projected," *Des Moines Register*, March 18, 1986, p. 1A.
4 This is the language of the Hatch Act, United States Code, Section 361b.
5 Ruskin, *Unto This Last*, p, 16.
6 *Familiar Letters of Henry David Thoreau*, ed. F. B. Sanborn (Boston and New York: Houghton Mifflin, 1894), p. 9.

What Are People For?

∞

Since World War II, the governing agricultural doctrine in government offices, universities, and corporations has been that "there are
too many people on the farm." This idea has supported, if indeed it
has not caused, one of the most consequential migrations of history:
millions of rural people moving from country to city in a stream that
has not slackened from the war's end until now. And the strongest
force behind this migration, then as now, has been economic ruin on
the farm. Today, with hundreds of farm families losing their farms
every week, the economists are still saying, as they have said all along,
that these people deserve to fail, that they have failed because they
are the "least efficient producers," and that the rest of us are better off
for their failure.

It is apparently easy to say that there are too many farmers, if one
is not a farmer. This is not a pronouncement often heard in farm

communities. Nor have farmers yet been informed of a dangerous surplus of population in the "agribusiness" professions or among the middlemen of the food system. No agricultural economist has yet perceived that there are too many agricultural economists.

The farm-to-city migration has obviously produced advantages to the corporate economy. The absent farmers have had to be replaced by machinery, petroleum, chemicals, credit, and other expensive goods and services from the agribusiness economy, which ought not to be confused with the economy of what used to be called farming.

But these short-term advantages all imply long-term disadvantages, to both country and city. The departure of so many people has seriously weakened rural communities and economies all over the country. And that our farmland no longer has enough caretakers is implied by the fact that, as the farming people have departed from the land, the land itself has departed. Our soil erosion rates are now higher than they were in the time of the Dust Bowl.

At the same time, the cities have had to receive a great influx of people unprepared for urban life and unable to cope with it. A friend of mine, a psychologist who has frequently worked with the juvenile courts in a large Midwestern city, has told me that a major occupation of the police force there is to keep the "permanently unemployable" confined in their own part of town. Such a circumstance cannot be good for the future of democracy and freedom. One wonders what the authors of our Constitution would have thought of that category, "permanently unemployable."

Equally important is the question of the sustainability of the urban food supply. The supermarkets are, at present, crammed with food, and the productivity of American agriculture is, at present, enormous. But this is a productivity based on the ruin both of the producers and of the source of production. City people are unworried about this, apparently, only because they do not know anything about farming. People who know about farming, who know what the farmland requires to remain productive, *are* worried. When topsoil losses exceed the weight of grain harvested fivefold (in Iowa) or twentyfold (in the wheat-lands of eastern Washington), there is something to worry about.

When the "too many" of the country arrive in the city, they are not called "too many." In the city they are called "unemployed" or "permanently unemployable." But what will happen if the economists ever perceive that there are too many people in the cities? There appear to be only two possibilities: Either they will have to recognize that their earlier diagnosis was a tragic error, or they will conclude that there are too many people in country and city both—and what further inhumanities will be justified by *that* diagnosis?

The great question that hovers over this issue, one that we have dealt with mainly by indifference, is the question of what people are *for*. Is their greatest dignity in unemployment? Is the obsolescence of human beings now our social goal? One would conclude so from our attitude toward work, especially the manual work necessary to the long-term preservation of the land, and from our rush toward mechanization, automation, and computerization. In a country that puts an absolute premium on labor-saving measures, short workdays, and retirement, why should there be any surprise at permanence of unemployment and welfare dependency? Those are only different names for our national ambitions.

In the country, meanwhile, there is work to be done. This is the inescapably necessary work of restoring and caring for our farms, forests, and rural towns and communities—work that we have not been able to pay people to do for forty years and that, thanks to our forty-year "solution to the farm problem," few people any longer know how to do.

(1985)

A Practical Harmony

∞

In 1913, seventy-five years ago, Liberty Hyde Bailey retired from his post at Cornell after a quarter-century during which he had been, first, Professor of Horticulture, and then Director and Dean of the New York State College of Agriculture and Director of the Experiment Station. Two years later he published a little book with the remarkable title *The Holy Earth*. In it he wrote: "Most of our difficulty with the earth lies in the effort to do what perhaps ought not to be done. . . . A good part of agriculture is to learn how to adapt one's work to nature. . . . To live in right relation with his natural conditions is one of the first lessons that a wise farmer or any other wise man learns."[1]

Was that perhaps the exhalation of a restless soul, having cast off at last its academic bonds? No, it was not. For in 1905, the second year of his deanship, he had published a book entitled *The Outlook to Nature*, in which he spoke of nature as "the norm." "If nature is the norm," he wrote, "then the necessity for correcting and amending the abuses of civilization becomes baldly apparent by very contrast." And he added, "The return to nature affords the very means of acquiring the incentive and energy for ambitious and constructive work of a high order." [2]

Dean Bailey was not, of course, against the necessary pursuits of the human economy. He was merely for bringing those pursuits into harmony with nature, which he understood as their source and pattern. I mention him here not just because he is one of the inevitable measures of the subsequent history of the land-grant system, but because, as an officer of that system, he spoke for a view of things that, however threatened in his time and since, goes back to the roots of our experience as human beings.

This view of things holds that we can live only in and from nature, and that we have, therefore, an inescapable obligation to be nature's students and stewards and to live in harmony with her. This is a theme of both the classical and the biblical traditions. It is not so prominent a theme as we could wish, perhaps because until lately it was taken for granted, but it is a constant theme, and it is more prominent than modern education prepares us to expect. Virgil, for example, states it boldly at the beginning of *The Georgics*, written between 36 and 29 B.C.:

> *. . . before we plow an unfamiliar patch*
> *It is well to be informed about the winds,*
> *About the variations in the sky,*
> *The native traits and habits of the place,*
> *What each locale permits, and what denies.*[3]

And several hundred years before that Job, the man of Uz, had said to his visitors:

> *. . . ask now the beasts, and they shall teach thee; and the*
> *fowls of the air, and they shall tell thee:*

Or speak to the earth, and it shall teach thee: and the
fishes of the sea shall declare unto thee.

In the English poetic tradition this theme is restated by voice after voice. Edmund Spenser, toward the end of the sixteenth century, described Nature as "the equall mother" of all creatures, who "knittest each to each, as brother unto brother." For that reason, perhaps, he sees her also as the instructor of creatures and the ultimate earthly judge of their behavior.

The theme was stated again by Shakespeare in *As You Like It*, in which the forest performs the role of teacher and judge, a role that is explicitly acknowledged by Touchstone: "You have said; but whether wisely or no, let the forest judge." And Milton stated the theme, again forthrightly, in *Comus*, when the Lady says of Nature:

> *she, good cateress,*
> *Means her provision only to the good*
> *That live according to her sober laws*
> *And holy dictate of spare Temperance.*

And Alexander Pope stated it, as plainly as the others, in his *Epistle to Burlington*, in which he counseled gardeners to "let Nature never be forgot" and to "Consult the Genius of the Place in all."

After Pope, so far as I know, this theme departs from English poetry. Later poets were inclined to see nature and humankind as radically divided and were no longer much interested in the issues of a *practical* harmony between the land and its human inhabitants. The romantic poets, who subscribed to the modern doctrine of the preeminence of the human mind, tended to look upon nature not as anything they might ever have practical dealings with, but as a reservoir of symbols.

The theme of nature as instructor and judge seems to have been taken up next by a series of agricultural writers in our own century.

I say "series" rather than "succession" because I don't know to what extent these people have worked consciously under the influence of predecessors. I suspect that the succession, in both poetry and agriculture, may lie in the familial and communal handing down of the agrarian common culture, rather than in any succession of teachers and students in the literary culture or in the schools. I do not, for example, know the ancestry of the mind of Liberty Hyde Bailey, though I would guess with some confidence that he is one of the heirs of Thomas Jefferson. Jefferson's preoccupation with what he called "horizontal plowing" and other issues of proper husbandry was certainly an attempt of a "wise farmer" to farm "in right relation to his natural conditions." But such a coincidence of thoughts does not establish succession. There remains the possibility—and I think it is a strong one—that, though Bailey undoubtedly knew the example of Jefferson, both men worked out of predisposing ideas and assumptions handed down to them as children.

One of Liberty Hyde Bailey's contemporaries was J. Russell Smith, whose interests and loyalties as an academician will seem as improbable to us as those of Dean Bailey. In 1929, when he was professor of economic geography at Columbia University, J. Russell Smith published a book entitled *Tree Crops*, the aims of which were at once ecological and patriotic. The book, he said, was "written to persons of imagination who love trees and love their country." His concern was the destruction of the hill lands by agriculture: "Man has carried to the hills the agriculture of the flat plain." Smith's answer to this problem was that "*farming should fit the land*." "Trees," he wrote, "are the natural crop plants for all such places." The great virtue of trees is that they are perennials; a hillside planted in trees would be "a permanent institution." Tree crops, he believed, could restore both the ecological and the human health of the hilly land. His vision was this:

> I see a million hills green with crop-yielding trees and a million neat farm homes snuggled in the hills. These beautiful tree

farms hold the hills from Boston to Austin, from Atlanta to Des Moines. The hills of my vision have farming that fits them and replaces the poor pasture, the gullies, and the abandoned lands that characterize today so large a part of these hills.

That J. Russell Smith was aware of the early work of Albert Howard we know from a footnote in *Tree Crops*. Whether or not Howard knew Smith's work, I do not know. Nevertheless, when Sir Albert Howard (as he came to be) published *An Agricultural Testament* in 1940, his message was essentially the same as Smith's (and essentially the same as that of the Book of Job, Virgil, Spenser, Shakespeare, Milton, Pope, and Liberty Hyde Bailey). Nature, he said, is "the supreme farmer." If one wants to know how to farm well, one must study the forest. In a paragraph as allegorical as *The Faerie Queene*, he wrote:

> The main characteristic of Nature's farming can therefore be summed up in a few words. Mother earth never attempts to farm without live stock; she always raises mixed crops; great pains are taken to preserve the soil and to prevent erosion; the mixed vegetable and animal wastes are converted into humus; there is no waste; the processes of growth and the processes of decay balance one another; ample provision is made to maintain large reserves of fertility; the greatest care is taken to store the rainfall; both plants and animals are left to protect themselves against disease.

Sir Albert Howard mentioned the prairie on the same page with the passage I just quoted, but he was native to country that was by nature forest land. It remained for Wes and Dana Jackson and their fellow workers at the Land Institute to take the logical next step to the proposition that if one lives on the prairie, one must learn to farm by studying the prairie. The difference between the native prairie and the modern grainfield is a critical one, and it provides the only feasible basis for criticism and correction of the grainfield. The principle is stated by Wes in Chapter 8 of *New Roots for Agriculture*: "The agricultural human's pull historically has been toward the monoculture of annuals. Nature's pull is toward a polyculture of perennials."

If the work of the Land Institute is innovative, it is so partly in response to a long tradition and an old hope. It is not merely another episode in our time's random pursuit of novelty. The Institute's purpose, as set forth by Wes Jackson and Marty Bender in their article "Investigations into Perennial Polyculture," is at once new and recognizably ancient: "We believe that the best agriculture for any region is the one that best mimics the region's natural ecosystems. . . . Our goal is . . . to create prairielike grain fields."

The goal is a harmony between the human economy and nature that will preserve both nature and humanity, and this is a traditional goal. The world is now divided between those who adhere to this ancient purpose and those who by intention do not—a division that is of far more portent for the future of the world than any of the presently recognized national or political or economic divisions.

The remarkable thing about this division is its relative newness. The idea that we should obey nature's laws and live harmoniously with her as good husbanders and stewards of her gifts is old. And I believe that until fairly recently our destructions of nature were more or less unwitting—the by-products, so to speak, of our ignorance or weakness or depravity. It is our present principled and elaborately rationalized rape and plunder of the natural world that is a new thing under the sun.

(1988)

NOTES
1 *The Holy Earth*, reprinted by The Christian Rural Fellowship, 1946, p. 9.
2 *The Outlook to Nature*, Macmillan, 1905, p. 8.
3 Translation by Smith Palmer Bovie, The University of Chicago Press, 1966, p. 5.

Two Economies

∞

I

Some time ago, in a conversation with Wes Jackson in which we were laboring to define the causes of the modern ruination of farmland, we finally got around to the money economy. I said that an economy based on energy would be more benign because it would be more comprehensive.

Wes would not agree. "An energy economy still wouldn't be comprehensive enough."

"Well," I said, "then what kind of economy *would* be comprehensive enough?"

He hesitated a moment, and then, grinning, said, "The Kingdom of God."

I assume that Wes used the term because he found it, at that point in our conversation, indispensable; I assume so because, in my pondering over its occurrence at that point, I have found it indispensable myself. For the thing that troubles us about the industrial economy is exactly that it is not comprehensive enough, that, moreover, it tends to destroy what it does not comprehend, and that it is *dependent* upon much that it does not comprehend. In attempting to criticize such an economy, we naturally pose against it an economy that does not leave anything out, and we can say without presuming too much that the first principle of the Kingdom of God is that it includes everything; in it, the fall of every sparrow is a significant event. We are in it whether we know it or not and whether we wish to be or not. Another principle, both ecological and traditional, is that everything in the Kingdom of God is joined both to it and to everything else that is in it; that is to say, the Kingdom of God is orderly. A third principle is that humans do not and can never know either all the creatures that the Kingdom of God contains or the whole pattern or order by which it contains them.

The suitability of the Kingdom of God as, so to speak, a place name is partly owing to the fact that it still means pretty much what it has always meant. Because, I think, of the embarrassment that the phrase has increasingly caused among the educated, it has not been much tainted or tampered with by the disinterested processes of academic thought; it is a phrase that comes to us with its cultural strings still attached. To say that we live in the Kingdom of God is both to suggest the difficulty of our condition and to imply a fairly complete set of culture-borne instructions for living in it. These instructions are not always explicitly ecological, but it can be argued that they are always implicitly so, for all of them rest ultimately on the assumptions that I have given as the second and third principles of the Kingdom of God: that we live within order and that this order is both greater and more intricate than we can know. The difficulty of our predicament, then, is made clear if we add a fourth principle: Though we cannot produce a complete or even an adequate description of this order, severe penalties are in store for us if we presume upon it or violate it.

I am not dealing, of course, with perceptions that are only biblical. The ancient Greeks, according to Aubrey de Sélincourt, saw "a continuing moral pattern in the vicissitudes of human fortune," a pattern "formed from the belief that men, as men, are subject to certain limitations imposed by a Power—call it Fate or God—which they cannot fully comprehend, and that any attempt to transcend those limitations is met by inevitable punishment."[1] The Greek name for the pride that attempts to transcend human limitations was "hubris," and hubris was the cause of what the Greeks understood as tragedy.

Nearly the same sense of *necessary* human limitation is implied in the Old Testament's repeated remonstrances against too great a human confidence in the power of "mine own hand." Gideon's army against the Midianites, for example, was reduced from thirty-two thousand to three hundred expressly to prevent the Israelites from saying, "Mine own hand hath saved me."[2] A similar purpose was served by the institution of the Sabbath, when, by not working, the Israelites were meant to see the limited efficacy of their work and thus to understand their true dependence.

Though I hope that my insistence on the usefulness of the term the Kingdom of God will be understood, I must acknowledge that the term is local, in the sense that it is fully available only to those whose languages are involved in Western or biblical tradition. A person of Eastern heritage, for example, might speak of the totality of all creation, visible and invisible, as "the Tao." I am well aware also that many people would not willingly use either term, or any such term. For these reasons, I do not want to make a statement that is specially or exclusively biblical, and so I would like now to introduce a more culturally neutral term for that economy that I have been calling the Kingdom of God. Sometimes, in thinking about it, I have called it the Great Economy, which is the name I am going to make do with here—though I will remain under the personal necessity of biblical reference. And that, I think, must be one of my points: We can name it whatever we wish, but we cannot define it except by way of a religious tradition. The Great Economy, like the Tao or the Kingdom of God, is both known and unknown, visible and invisible, comprehensible and mysterious. It is, thus, the ultimate condition of our experience and of the practical questions rising from our experience, and it imposes on our consideration of those questions an extremity of seriousness and an extremity of humility.

I am assuming that the Great Economy, whatever we may name it, is indeed—and in ways that are, to some extent, practical—an economy: It includes principles and patterns by which values or powers or necessities are parceled out and exchanged. But if the Great Economy comprehends humans and thus cannot be fully comprehended by them, then it is also not an economy in which humans can participate directly. What this suggests, in fact, is that humans can live in the Great Economy only with great uneasiness, subject to powers and laws that they can understand only in part. There is no human accounting for the Great Economy. This obviously is a description of the circumstance of religion, the circumstance that *causes* religion. De Sélincourt states the problem succinctly: "Religion in every age is concerned with the vast and fluctuant regions of experience which knowledge cannot penetrate, the regions which a man knows, or feels, to stretch away beyond the narrow, closed circle of what he can *manage* by the use of his wits." [3]

If there is no denying our dependence on the Great Economy, there is also no denying our need for a little economy—a narrow circle within which things are manageable by the use of our wits. I don't think Wes Jackson was denying this need when he invoked the Kingdom of God as the complete economy; rather, he was, I think, insisting upon a priority that is both proper and practical. If he had a text in mind, it must have been the sixth chapter of Matthew, in which, after speaking of God's care for nature, the fowls of the air and the lilies of the field, Jesus says: "Therefore take no thought, saying, What shall we eat? or, What shall we drink? or, Wherewithal shall we be clothed? ... But seek ye first the kingdom of God, and his righteousness; and all these things shall be added unto you." [4]

There is an attitude that sees in this text a denial of the value of *any* economy of this world, but this attitude makes the text useless and meaningless to humans who must live in this world. These verses make usable sense only if we read them as a statement of considerable practical import about the real nature of worldly economy. If this passage meant for us to seek *only* the Kingdom of God, it would have the odd result of making good people not only feckless but also dependent upon bad people busy with quite other seekings. It says, rather, to seek the Kingdom of God *first*; that is, it gives an obviously necessary priority to the Great Economy over any little economy made within it. The passage also clearly includes nature within the Great Economy, and it affirms the goodness, indeed the sanctity, of natural creatures.

The fowls of the air and the lilies of the field live within the Great Economy entirely by nature, whereas humans, though entirely dependent upon it, must live in it partly by artifice. The birds can live in the Great Economy only as birds, the flowers only as flowers, the humans only as humans. The humans, unlike the wild creatures, may choose not to live in it—or, rather, since no creature can escape it, they may choose to *act* as if they do not, or they may choose to try to live in it on their own terms. If humans choose to live in the Great Economy on *its* terms, then they must live in harmony with it, maintaining it in trust and learning to consider the lives of the wild creatures.

Certain economic restrictions are clearly implied, and these restrictions have mainly to do with the economics of futurity. We know from other passages in the Gospels that a certain preparedness or provisioning for the future is required of us. It may be that such preparedness is part of our obligation to today, and for *that* reason we need "take no thought for the morrow." [5] But it is clear that such preparations can be carried too far, that we can provide too much for the future. The sin of "a certain rich man" in the twelfth chapter of Luke is that he has "much goods laid up for many years" and thus believes that he can "eat, drink, and be merry." [6] The offense seems to be that he has stored up too much and in the process has belittled the future, for he has reduced it to the size of his own hopes and expectations. He is prepared for a future in which he will be prosperous, not for one in which he will be dead. We know from our own experience that it is possible to live in the present in such a way as to diminish the future practically as well as spiritually. By laying up "much goods" in the present—and, in the process, *using up* such goods as topsoil, fossil fuel, and fossil water—we incur a debt to the future that we cannot repay. That is, we diminish the future by deeds that we call "use" but that the future will call "theft." We may say, then, that we seek the Kingdom of God, in part, by our economic behavior, and we fail to find it if that behavior is wrong.

If we read Matthew 6:24–34 as a teaching that is *both* practical and spiritual, as I think we must, then we must see it as prescribing the terms of a kind of little economy or human economy. Since I am deriving it here from a Christian text, we could call it a Christian economy. But we need not call it that. A Buddhist might look at the working principles of the economy I am talking about and call it a Buddhist economy. E. F. Schumacher, in fact, says that the aim of "Buddhist economics" is "to obtain the maximum of well-being with the minimum of consumption," [7] which I think is partly the sense of Matthew 6:24–34. Or we could call this economy (from Matthew 6:28) a "considerate" economy or, simply, a good economy. Whatever the name, the human economy, if it is to be a good economy, must fit harmoniously within and must correspond to the Great Economy; in certain important ways, it must be an analogue of the Great Economy.

A fifth principle of the Great Economy that must now be added to the previous four is that *we* cannot foresee an end to it: The same basic stuff is going to be shifting from one form to another, so far as we know, forever. From a human point of view, this is a rather heartless endurance. As cynics sometimes point out, conservation is always working, for what is lost or wasted in one place always turns up someplace else. Thus, soil erosion in Iowa involves no loss because the soil is conserved in the Gulf of Mexico. Such people like to point out that soil erosion is as "natural" as birdsong. And so it is, though these people neglect to observe that soil conservation is also natural, and that, before the advent of farming, nature alone worked effectively to keep Iowa topsoil in Iowa. But to say that soil erosion is natural is only a way of saying that there are some things that the Great Economy cannot do for humans. Only a little economy, only a good human economy, can define for us the value of keeping the topsoil where it is.

A good human economy, that is, defines and values human goods, and, like the Great Economy, it conserves and protects its goods. It proposes to endure. Like the Great Economy, a good human economy does not propose for itself a term to be set by humans. That termlessness, with all its implied human limits and restraints, is a human good.

The difference between the Great Economy and any human economy is pretty much the difference between the goose that laid the golden egg and the golden egg. For the goose to have value as a layer of golden eggs, she must be a live goose and therefore joined to the life cycle, which means that she is joined to all manner of things, patterns, and processes that sooner or later surpass human comprehension. The golden egg, on the other hand, can be fully valued by humans according to kind, weight, and measure—but it will not hatch, and it cannot be eaten. To make the value of the egg *fully* accountable, then, we must make it "golden," must remove it from life. But if in our valuation of it, we wish to consider its relation to the goose, we have to undertake a different kind of accounting, more exacting if less exact. That is, if we wish to value the egg in such a way as to preserve the goose that laid it, we find that we must behave, not scientifically, but humanely; we must understand ourselves as humans as fully as our traditional knowledge of ourselves permits. We participate in our little human economy to a considerable extent, that is, by factual knowledge, calculation, and manipulation; our participation in the Great Economy also requires those things, but requires as well humility, sympathy, forbearance, generosity, imagination.

Another critical difference, implicit in the foregoing, is that, though a human economy can evaluate, distribute, use, and preserve things of value, it cannot make value. Value can originate only in the Great Economy. It is true enough that humans can add value to natural things: We may transform trees into boards, and transform boards into chairs, adding value at each transformation. In a good human economy, these transformations would be made by good work, which would be properly valued and the workers properly rewarded. But a good human economy would recognize at the same time that it was dealing all along with materials and powers that it did not make. It did not make trees, and it did not make the intelligence and talents of the human workers. What the humans have added at every step is artificial, made by art, and though the value of art is critical to human life, it is a secondary value.

When humans presume to originate value, they make value that is first abstract and then false, tyrannical, and destructive of real value. Money value, for instance, can be said to be true only when it justly and stably represents the value of necessary goods, such as clothing, food, and shelter, which originate ultimately in the Great Economy. Humans can originate money value in the abstract, but only by inflation and usury, which falsify the value of necessary things and damage their natural and human sources. Inflation and usury and the damages that follow can be understood, perhaps, as retributions for the presumption that humans can make value.

. . .

We may say, then, that a human economy originates, manages, and distributes secondary or added values but that, if it is to last long, it must also manage in such a way as to make continuously available those values that are primary or given, the secondary values having mainly to do with husbandry and trusteeship. A little economy is obliged to receive them gratefully and to use them in such a way as not to diminish them. We might make a long list of things that we would have to describe as primary values, which come directly into the little economy from the Great, but the one I want to talk about, because it is the one with which we have the most intimate working relationship, is the topsoil.

We cannot speak of topsoil, indeed we cannot know what it is without acknowledging at the outset that we cannot make it. We can care for it (or not), we can even, as we say, "build" it, but we can do so only by assenting to, preserving, and perhaps collaborating in its own processes. To those processes themselves we have nothing to contribute. We cannot make topsoil, and we cannot make any substitute for it; we cannot do what it does. It is apparently impossible to make an adequate description of topsoil in the sort of language that we have come to call "scientific." For, although any soil sample can be reduced to its inert quantities, a handful of the real thing has life in it; it is full of living creatures. And if we try to describe the behavior of that life we will see that it is doing something that, if we are not careful, we will call "unearthly": It is making life out of death. Not so very long ago, had we known about it what we know now, we would probably have called it "miraculous." In a time when death is looked upon with almost universal enmity, it is hard to believe that the land we live on and the lives we live are the gifts of death. Yet that is so, and it is the topsoil that makes it so. In fact, in talking about topsoil, it is hard to avoid the language of religion. When, in "This Compost," Whitman says, "The resurrection of the wheat appears with pale visage out of its graves," he is speaking in the Christian tradition, and yet he is describing what happens, with language that is entirely accurate and appropriate. And when at last he says of the earth that "It gives such divine materials to men," we feel that the propriety of the words comes not from convention but from the actuality of the uncanny transformation that his poem has required us to imagine, as if in obedience to the summons to "consider the lilies of the field."

Even in its functions that may seem, to mechanists, to be mechanical, the topsoil behaves complexly and wonderfully. A healthy topsoil, for instance, has at once the ability to hold water and to drain well. When we speak of the health of a watershed, these abilities are what we are talking about, and the word "health," which we do use in speaking of watersheds, warns us that we are not speaking merely of mechanics. A healthy soil is made by the life dying into it and by the life living in it, and to its double ability to drain and retain water we are complexly indebted, for it not only gives us good crops but also erosion control as well as *both* flood control and a constant water supply.

Obviously, topsoil, not energy or money, is the critical quantity in agriculture. And topsoil *is* a quantity; we need it in quantities. We now need more of it than we have; we need to help it to make more of itself. But it is a most peculiar quantity, for it is inseparable from quality. Topsoil is by definition *good* soil, and it can be preserved in human use only by good care. When humans see it as a mere quantity, they tend to make it that; they destroy the life in it, and they begin to measure in inches and feet and tons how much of it they have "lost."

When we see the topsoil as the foundation of that household of living creatures and their nonliving supports that we now call an "ecosystem" but which some of us understand better as a "neighborhood," we find ourselves in debt for other benefits that baffle our mechanical logic and defy our measures. For example, one of the principles of an ecosystem is that diversity increases capacity—or, to put it another way, that complications of form or pattern can increase greatly within quantitative limits. I suppose that this may be true only up to a point, but I suppose also that that point is far beyond the human capacity to understand or diagram the pattern.

On a farm put together on a sound ecological pattern, the same principle holds. Henry Besuden, the great farmer and shepherd of Clark County, Kentucky, compares the small sheep flock to the two spoons of sugar that can be added to a brimful cup of coffee, which then becomes "more palatable [but] doesn't run over. You can stock your farm to the limit with other livestock and still add a small flock of sheep." He says this, characteristically, after rejecting the efforts of sheep specialists to get beyond "the natural physical limits of the ewe" by breeding out of season in order to get three lamb crops in two years or by striving for "litters" of lambs rather than nature's optimum of twins. Rather than chafe at "natural physical limits," he would turn to nature's elegant way of enriching herself *within* her physical limits by diversification, by complication of pattern. Rather than strain the productive capacity of the ewe, he would, without strain, enlarge the productive capacity of the farm—a healthier, safer, and cheaper procedure. Like many of the better traditional farmers, Henry Besuden is suspicious of "the measure of land in length and width," for he would be mindful as well of "the depth and quality." [8]

A small flock of ewes, fitted properly into a farm's pattern, virtually disappears into the farm and does it good, just as it virtually disappears into the time and energy economy of a farm family and does it good. And, properly fitted into the farm's pattern, the small flock virtually disappears from the debit side of the farm's accounts but shows up plainly on the credit side. This "disappearance" is possible, not to the extent that the farm is a human artifact, a belonging of the human economy, but to the extent that it remains, by its obedience to natural principle, a belonging of the Great Economy.

A little economy may be said to be good insofar as it perceives the excellence of these benefits and husbands and preserves them. It is by holding up this standard of goodness that we can best see what is wrong with the industrial economy. For the industrial economy does not see itself as a little economy; it sees itself as the *only* economy. It makes itself thus exclusive by the simple expedient of valuing only what it can use—that is, only what it can regard as "raw material" to be transformed mechanically into something else. What it cannot use, it characteristically describes as "useless," "worthless," "random," or "wild," and gives it some such name as "chaos," "disorder," or "waste"—and thus ruins it or cheapens it in preparation for eventual use. That western deserts or eastern mountains were once perceived as "useless" made it easy to dignify them by the "use" of strip mining. Once we acknowledge the existence of the Great Economy, however, we are astonished and frightened to see how much modern enterprise is the work of hubris, occurring outside the human boundary established by ancient tradition. The industrial economy is based on invasion and pillage of the Great Economy.

The weakness of the industrial economy is clearly revealed when it imposes its terms upon agriculture, for its terms cannot define those natural principles that are most vital to the life and longevity of farms. Even if the industrial economists could afford to do so, they could not describe the dependence of agriculture upon nature. If asked to consider the lilies of the field or told that the wheat is resurrected out of its graves, the agricultural industrialist would reply that "my engineer's mind inclines less toward the poetic and philosophical, and more toward the practical and possible," [9] unable even to suspect that such a division of mind induces blindness to possibilities of the utmost practical concern.

That good topsoil both drains and retains water, that diversity increases capacity, are facts similarly alien to industrial logic. Industrialists see retention and drainage as different and opposite functions, and they would promote one at the expense of the other, just as, diversity being inimical to industrial procedure, they would commit themselves to the forlorn expedient of enlarging capacity by increasing area. They are thus encumbered by dependence on mechanical solutions that can work only by isolating and oversimplifying problems. Industrialists are condemned to proceed by devices. To facilitate water retention, they must resort to a specialized water-holding device such as a terrace or a dam; to facilitate drainage, they must use drain tile, or a ditch, or a "subsoiler." It is possible, I know, to argue that this analysis is too general and to produce exceptions, but I do not think it deniable that the discipline of soil conservation is now principally that of the engineer, not that of the farmer or soil husband—that it is now a matter of digging in the earth, not of enriching it.

I do not mean to say that the devices of engineering are always inappropriate; they have their place, not least in the restoration of land abused by the devices of engineering. My point is that, to facilitate both water retention and drainage in the same place, we must improve the soil, which is not a mechanical device but, among other things, a graveyard, a place of resurrection, and a community of living creatures. Devices may sometimes help, but only up to a point, for soil is improved by what humans do not do as well as by what they do. The proprieties of soil husbandry require acts that are much more complex than industrial acts, for these acts are conditioned by the ability *not* to act, by forbearance or self-restraint, sympathy or generosity. The industrial act is simply prescribed by thought, but the act of soil building is also *limited* by thought. We build soil by knowing what to do but also by knowing what not to do and by knowing when to stop. Both kinds of knowledge are necessary because invariably, at some point, the reach of human comprehension becomes too short, and at that point the work of the human economy must end in absolute deference to the working of the Great Economy. This, I take it, is the practical significance of the idea of the Sabbath.

To push our work beyond that point, invading the Great Economy, is to become guilty of hubris, of presuming to be greater than we are. We cannot do what the topsoil does, any more than we can do what God does or what a swallow does. We can fly, but only as humans— very crudely, noisily, and clumsily. We can dispose of corpses and gar- bage, but we cannot, by our devices, turn them into fertility and new life. And we are discovering, to our great uneasiness, that we cannot dispose at all of some of our so-called wastes that are toxic or radio- active. We can appropriate and in some fashion use godly powers, but we cannot use them safely, and we cannot control the results. That is to say that the human condition remains for us what it was for Homer and the authors of the Bible. Now that we have brought such enormous powers to our aid (we hope), it seems more necessary than ever to observe how inexorably the human condition still contains us. We only do what humans can do, and our machines, however they may appear to enlarge our possibilities, are invariably infected with our limitations. Sometimes, in enlarging our possibilities, they narrow our limits and leave us more powerful but less content, less safe, and less free. The mechanical means by which we propose to escape the human condition only extend it; thinking to transcend our definition as fallen creatures, we have only colonized more and more territory eastward of Eden.

II

Like the rich man of the parable, the industrialist thinks to escape the persistent obligations of the human condition by means of "much goods laid up for many years"—by means, in other words, of quanti- ties: resources, supplies, stockpiles, funds, reserves. But this is a grossly oversimplifying dream and, thus, a dangerous one. All the great natural goods that empower agriculture, some of which I have discussed, have to do with quantities, but they have to do also with qualities, and they involve principles that are not static but active; they have to do with formal processes. The topsoil exists as such because it is ceaselessly transforming death into life, ceaselessly supplying food and water to all that lives in it and from it; otherwise, "All flesh shall perish together, and man shall turn again unto dust." [10] If we are to live well on and from our land, we must live by faith in the ceaselessness of these processes and by faith in our own willingness and ability to collaborate with them. Christ's prayer for "daily bread" is an affirmation of such faith, just as it is a repudiation of faith in "much goods laid up." Our life and livelihood are the gift of the topsoil and of our willingness and ability to care for it, to grow good wheat, to make good bread; they do not derive from stockpiles of raw materials or accumulations of purchasing power.

The industrial economy can define potentiality, even the potentiality of the living topsoil, only as a *fund*, and thus it must accept impoverishment as the inescapable condition of abundance. The invariable mode of its relation both to nature and to human culture is that of mining: withdrawal from a limited fund until that fund is exhausted. It removes natural fertility and human workmanship from the land, just as it removes nourishment and human workmanship from bread. Thus the land is reduced to abstract marketable quantities of length and width, and bread to merchandise that is high in money value but low in food value. "Our bread," Guy Davenport once said to me, "is more obscene than our movies."

But the industrial use of *any* "resource" implies its exhaustion. It is for this reason that the industrial economy has been accompanied by an ever-increasing hurry of research and exploration, the motive of which is not "free enterprise" or "the spirit of free inquiry," as industrial scientists and apologists would have us believe, but the desperation that naturally and logically accompanies gluttony.

One of the favorite words of the industrial economy is "control": We want "to keep things under control"; we wish (or so we say) to "control" inflation and erosion; we have a discipline known as "crowd control"; we believe in "controlled growth" and "controlled development,"

in "traffic control" and "self-control." But, because we are always setting out to control something that we refuse to limit, we have made
control a permanent and a helpless enterprise. If we will not limit
causes, there can be no controlling of effects. What is to be the fate of
self-control in an economy that encourages and rewards unlimited
selfishness?

More than anything else, we would like to "control the forces of
nature," refusing at the same time to impose any limit on human
nature. We assume that such control and such freedom are our
"rights," which seems to ensure that our means of control (of nature
and of all else that we see as alien) will be violent. It is startling to
recognize the extent to which the industrial economy depends upon
controlled explosions—in mines, in weapons, in the cylinders of
engines, in the economic pattern known as "boom and bust." This
dependence is the result of a progress that can be argued for, but those
who argue for it must recognize that, in all these means, good ends
are served by a destructive principle, an association that is difficult
to control if it is not limited; moreover, they must recognize that our
failure to limit this association has raised the specter of uncontrollable
explosion. Nuclear holocaust, if it comes, will be the final detonation
of an explosive economy.

An explosive economy, then, is not only an economy that is dependent upon explosions but also one that sets no limits on itself. Any
little economy that sees itself as unlimited is obviously self-blinded.
It does not see its real relation of dependence and obligation to the
Great Economy; in fact, it does not see that there *is* a Great Economy. Instead, it calls the Great Economy "raw material" or "natural
resources" or "nature" and proceeds with the business of putting it
"under control."

But "control" is a word more than ordinarily revealing here, for
its root meaning is to roll against, in the sense of a little wheel turning in opposition. The principle of control, then, involves necessarily

the principle of division: One thing may turn against another thing only by being divided from it. This mechanical division and turning in opposition William Blake understood as evil, and he spoke of "Satanic wheels" and "Satanic mills": "wheel without wheel, with cogs tyrannic / Moving by compulsion each other." [11] By "wheel without wheel," Blake meant wheel outside of wheel, one wheel communicating motion to the other in the manner of two cogwheels, the point being that one wheel can turn another wheel outside itself only in a direction opposite to its own. This, I suppose, is acceptable enough as a mechanism. It becomes "Satanic" when it becomes a ruling metaphor and is used to describe and to organize fundamental relationships. Against the Satanic "wheel without wheel," Blake set the wheels of Eden, which "Wheel within wheel in freedom revolve, in harmony and peace." [12] This is the "wheel in the middle of a wheel" [13] of Ezekiel's vision, and it is an image of harmony. That the relation of these wheels is not mechanical we know from Ezekiel 1:21: "the spirit of the living creature was in the wheels." The wheels of opposition oppose the spirit of the living creature.

What had happened, as Blake saw accurately and feared justifiably, was a fundamental shift in the relation of humankind to the rest of creation. Sometime between, say, Pope's verses on the Chain of Being in *An Essay on Man* and Blake's "London," the dominant minds had begun to see the human race, not as a part or a member of Creation, but as outside it and opposed to it. The industrial revolution was only a part of this change, but it is true that, when the wheels of the industrial revolution began to revolve, they turned against nature, which became the name for all of Creation thought to be below humanity, as well as, incidentally, against all once thought to be above humanity. Perhaps this would have been safe enough if nature—that is, if all the rest of Creation—had been, as proposed, passively subject to human purpose.

Of course, it never has been. As Blake foresaw, and as we now know, what we turn against must turn against us. Blake's image of the cogwheels turning in relentless opposition is terrifyingly apt, for in our vaunted war against nature, nature fights back. The earth may answer our pinches and pokes "only with spring," [14] as e. e. cummings said, but if we pinch and poke too much, she can answer also with flood or drouth, with catastrophic soil erosion, with plague and famine. Many of the occurrences that we call "acts of God" or "accidents of nature" are simply forthright natural responses to human provocations. Not always; I do not mean to imply here that, by living in harmony with nature, we can be free of floods and storms and drouths and earthquakes and volcanic eruptions; I am only pointing out, as many others have done, that, by living in opposition to nature, we can *cause* natural calamities of which we would otherwise be free.

The problem seems to be that a human economy cannot prescribe the terms of its own success. In a time when we wish to believe that humans are the sole authors of the truth, that truth is relative, and that value judgments are all subjective, it is hard to say that a human economy can be wrong, and yet we have good, sound, practical reasons for saying so. It is indeed possible for a human economy to be wrong—not relatively wrong, in the sense of being "out of adjustment," or unfair according to some human definition of fairness, or weak according to the definition of its own purposes—but wrong absolutely and according to practical measures. Of course, if we see the human economy as the *only* economy, we will see its errors as political failures, and we will continue to talk about "recovery." It is only when we think of the little human economy in relation to the Great Economy that we begin to understand our errors for what they are and to see the qualitative meanings of our quantitative measures. If we see the industrial economy in terms of the Great Economy, then we begin to see industrial wastes and losses not as "trade-offs" or "necessary risks" but as costs that, like all costs, are chargeable to somebody, sometime.

That we can prescribe the terms of our own success, that we can live outside or in ignorance of the Great Economy are the greatest errors. They condemn us to a life without a standard, wavering in inescapable bewilderment from paltry self-satisfaction to paltry self-dissatisfaction. But since we have no place to live but in the Great Economy, whether or not we know that and act accordingly is the critical question, not about economy merely, but about human life itself.

It is possible to make a little economy, such as our present one, that is so short-sighted and in which accounting is of so short a term as to give the impression that vices are necessary and practically justifiable. When we make our economy a little wheel turning in opposition to what we call "nature," then we set up competitiveness as the ruling principle in our explanation of reality and in our understanding of economy; we make of it, willy-nilly, a virtue. But competitiveness, as a ruling principle and a virtue, imposes a logic that is extremely difficult, perhaps impossible, to control. That logic explains why our cars and our clothes are shoddily made, why our "wastes" are toxic, and why our "defensive" weapons are suicidal; it explains why it is so difficult for us to draw a line between "free enterprise" and crime. If our economic ideal is maximum profit with minimum responsibility, why should we be surprised to find our corporations so frequently in court and robbery on the increase? Why should we be surprised to find that medicine has become an exploitive industry, profitable in direct proportion to its hurry and its mechanical indifference? People who pay for shoddy products or careless services and people who are robbed outright are equally victims of theft, the only difference being that the robbers outright are not guilty of fraud.

If, on the other hand, we see ourselves as living within the Great Economy, under the necessity of making our little human economy within it, according to its terms, the smaller wheel turning in sympathy with the greater, receiving its being and its motion from it, then we see that the traditional virtues are necessary and are practically justifiable. Then, because in the Great Economy *all* transactions count and the account is never "closed," the ideal changes. We see that we cannot *afford* maximum profit or power with minimum responsibility because, in the Great Economy, the loser's losses finally afflict the winner. Now the ideal must be "the maximum of well-being with the minimum of consumption," which both defines and requires neighborly love. Competitiveness cannot be the ruling principle, for the Great Economy is not a "side" that we can join nor are there such "sides" within it. Thus, it is not the "sum of its parts" but a *membership* of parts inextricably joined to each other, indebted to each other, receiving significance and worth from each other and from the whole. One is obliged to "consider the lilies of the field," not because they are lilies or because they are exemplary, but because they are fellow members and because, as fellow members, we and the lilies are in certain critical ways alike.

To say that within the Great Economy the virtues are necessary and practically justifiable is at once to remove them from that specialized, sanctimonious, condescending practice of virtuousness that is humorless, pointless, and intolerable to its beneficiaries. For a human, the good choice in the Great Economy is to see its membership as a neighborhood and oneself as a neighbor within it. I am sure that virtues count in a neighborhood—to "love thy neighbor as thyself" requires the help of all seven of them—but I am equally sure that in a neighborhood the virtues cannot be practiced as such. Temperance has no appearance or action of its own, nor does justice, prudence, fortitude, faith, hope, or charity. They can only be employed on occasions. "He who would do good to another," William Blake said, "must do it in Minute Particulars." [15] To help each other, that is, we must go beyond the coldhearted charity of the "general good" and get down to work where we are:

> *Labour well the Minute Particulars, attend to the Little-ones,*
> *And those who are in misery cannot remain so long*
> *If we do but our duty: labour well the teeming Earth.* [16]

It is the Great Economy, not any little economy, that invests minute particulars with high and final importance. In the Great Economy, each part stands for the whole and is joined to it; the whole is present in the part and is its health. The industrial economy, by contrast, is always striving and failing to make fragments (pieces that *it* has broken) *add up* to an ever-fugitive wholeness.

Work that is authentically placed and understood within the Great Economy moves virtue toward virtuosity—that is, toward skill or technical competence. There is no use in helping our neighbors with their work if we do not know how to work. When the virtues are rightly practiced within the Great Economy, we do not call them virtues; we call them good farming, good forestry, good carpentry, good husbandry, good weaving and sewing, good homemaking, good parenthood, good neighborhood, and so on. The general principles are submerged in the particularities of their engagement with the world. Lao Tzu saw the appearance of the virtues as such, in the abstract, as indicative of their loss:

> *When people lost sight of the way to live*
> *Came codes of love and honesty . . .*
> *When differences weakened family ties*
> *Came benevolent fathers and dutiful sons;*
> *And when lands were disrupted and misgoverned*
> *Came ministers commended as loyal.*[17]

And these lines might be read as an elaboration of the warning against the *appearances* of goodness at the beginning of the sixth chapter of Matthew.

The work of the small economy, when it is understandingly placed within the Great Economy, minutely particularizes the virtues and carries principle into practice; to the extent that it does so, it escapes specialization. The industrial economy requires the extreme specialization of work—the separation of work from its results—because it

subsists upon divisions of interest and must deny the fundamental kinships of producer and consumer; seller and buyer; owner and worker;
worker, work, and product; parent material and product; nature and
artifice; thoughts, words, and deeds. Divided from those kinships,
specialized artists and scientists identify themselves as "observers" or
"objective observers"—that is, as outsiders without responsibility or
involvement. But the industrialized arts and sciences are false, their
division is a lie, for there is no specialization of results.

There is no "outside" to the Great Economy, no escape into either
specialization or generality, no "time off." Even insignificance is no
escape, for in the membership of the Great Economy everything
signifies; whatever we do counts. If we do not serve what coheres and
endures, we serve what disintegrates and destroys. We can *presume*
that we are outside the membership that includes us, but that presumption only damages the membership—and ourselves, of course,
along with it.

In the industrial economy, the arts and the sciences are specialized
"professions," each having its own language, speaking to none of the
others. But the Great Economy proposes arts and sciences of membership: ways of doing and ways of knowing that cannot be divided
from each other or within themselves and that speak the common
language of the communities where they are practiced.

(1988)

NOTES

1 Aubrey de Sélincourt, *The World of Herodotus* (San Francisco: North Point Press,
1982), p. 23.
2 Judges 7:2-21.
3 Sélincourt, *World of Herodotus*, p. 171.
4 Matt. 6:31, 33.
5 Matt. 6:34.

6 Luke 12:16-19.

7 E. F. Schumacher, *Small Is Beautiful* (New York: Harper & Row, 1973) p. 54.

8 Henry Besuden, Speech delivered to International Stockmen's School, San Antonio, Texas, January 2-6, 1983.

9 Gordon Millar, "Agriculture: Is Small Really Beautiful?" *World Research INK* (January 1978), p. 10.

10 Job 34:15

11 William Blake, *Jerusalem*, plate 15, lines 18-19.

12 Ibid., line 20.

13 Ezek. 1:16.

14 e.e. cummings, *Poems 1923-1954* (New York: Harcourt, Brace and Company, 1954), p. 39.

15 Blake, *Jerusalem*, plate 55, line 60.

16 Ibid., lines 51-53.

17 Lao Tzu, *The Way of Life (Too Teh Ching)*, trans. Witter Bynner (New York: Capricorn Books, 1962), p. 35.

The Work of Local Culture

∞

For many years, my walks have taken me down an old fencerow in a wooded hollow on what was once my grandfather's farm. A battered galvanized bucket is hanging on a fence post near the head of the hollow, and I never go by it without stopping to look inside. For what is going on in that bucket is the most momentous thing I know, the greatest miracle that I have ever heard of: It is making earth. The old bucket has hung there through many autumns, and the leaves have fallen around it and some have fallen into it. Rain and snow have fallen into it, and the fallen leaves have held the moisture and so have rotted. Nuts have fallen into it, or been carried into it by squirrels; mice and squirrels have eaten the meat of the nuts and left the shells; they and other animals have left their droppings; insects have flown into the bucket and died and decayed; birds have scratched in it and left their droppings or perhaps a feather or two. This slow work of growth and death, gravity and decay, which is the chief work of the world, has by now produced in the bottom of the bucket several inches of black humus. I look into that bucket with fascination because I am a farmer of sorts and an artist of sorts, and I recognize there an artistry and a farming far superior to mine, or to that of any human. I have seen the same process at work on the tops of boulders in a forest, and it has been at work immemorially over most of the land surface of the world. All creatures die into it, and they live by it.

The old bucket started out a far better one than you can buy now. I think it has been hanging on that post for something like fifty years. I think so because I remember hearing, when I was just a small boy, a story about a bucket that must have been this one. Several of my grandfather's black hired hands went out on an early spring day to burn a tobacco plant bed, and they took along some eggs to boil to eat with their dinner. When dinner time came and they looked around for something to boil the eggs in, they could find only an old bucket that at one time had been filled with tar. The boiling water softened the residue of tar, and one of the eggs came out of the water black. The hands made much sport of seeing who would have to eat the black egg, welcoming their laughter in the midst of their day's work. The man who had to eat the black egg was Floyd Scott, whom I remember well. Dry scales of tar still adhere to the inside of the bucket.

However small a landmark the old bucket is, it is not trivial. It is one of the signs by which I know my country and myself. And to me it is irresistibly suggestive in the way it collects leaves and other woodland sheddings as they fall through time. It collects stories, too, as they fall through time. It is irresistibly metaphorical. It is doing in a passive way what a human community must do actively and thought-fully. A human community, too, must collect leaves and stories, and turn them to account. It must build soil, and build that memory of itself—in lore and story and song—that will be its culture. These two kinds of accumulation, of local soil and local culture, are intimately related.

. . .

In the woods, the bucket is no metaphor; it simply reveals what is always happening in the woods, if the woods is let alone. Of course, in most places in my part of the country, the human community did not leave the woods alone. It felled the trees and replaced them with pastures and crops. But this did not revoke the law of the woods, which is that the ground must be protected by a cover of vegetation and that the growth of the years must return—or be returned—to the ground to rot and build soil. A good local culture, in one of its most important functions, is a collection of the memories, ways, and skills necessary for the observance, within the bounds of domesticity, of this natural law. If the local culture cannot preserve and improve the local soil, then, as both reason and history inform us, the local community will decay and perish, and the work of soil building will be resumed by nature.

A human community, then, if it is to last long, must exert a sort of centripetal force, holding local soil and local memory in place. Practically speaking, human society has no work more important than this. Once we have acknowledged this principle, we can only be alarmed at the extent to which it has been ignored. For although our present society does generate a centripetal force of great power, this is not a local force, but one centered almost exclusively in our great commercial and industrial cities, which have drawn irresistibly into themselves both the products of the countryside and the people and talents of the country communities.

There is, as one assumes there must be, a countervailing or cen-trifugal force that also operates in our society, but this returns to the countryside not the residue of the land's growth to refertilize the fields, not the learning and experience of the greater world ready to go to work locally, and not—or not often—even a just monetary compensation. What are returned, instead, are overpriced manufac-tured goods, pollution in various forms, and garbage. A landfill on the edge of my own rural county in Kentucky, for example, daily receives about eighty truckloads of garbage. Fifty to sixty of these loads come from cities in New York, New Jersey, and Pennsylvania. Thus, the end result of the phenomenal modern productivity of the countryside is a debased countryside, which becomes daily less pleasant, and which will inevitably become less productive.

The cities, which have imposed this inversion of forces on the country, have been unable to preserve themselves from it. The typical modern city is surrounded by a circle of affluent suburbs, eating its way outward, like ringworm, leaving the so-called inner city desolate, filthy, ugly, and dangerous.

My walks in the hills and hollows around my home have inevitably produced in my mind the awareness that I live in a diminished country. The country has been and is being reduced by the great centralizing process that is our national economy. As I walk, I am always reminded of the slow, patient building of soil in the woods. And I am reminded of the events and companions of my life—for my walks, after so long, are cultural events. But under the trees and in the fields I see also the gullies and scars, healed or healing or fresh, left by careless logging and bad farming. I see the crumbling stone walls and the wire fences that have been rusting out ever since the 1930s. In the returning woods growth of the hollows, I see the sagging and the fallen barns, the empty and ruining houses, the houseless chimneys and founda- tions. As I look at this evidence of human life poorly founded, played out, and gone, I try to recover some understanding, some vision, of what this country was at the beginning: the great oaks and beeches and hickories, walnuts and maples, lindens and ashes, tulip poplars, standing in beauty and dignity now unimaginable, the black soil of their making, also no longer imaginable, lying deep at their feet—an incalculable birthright sold for money, most of which we did not receive. Most of the money made on the products of this place has gone to fill the pockets of people in distant cities who did not produce the products.

If my walks take me along the roads and streams, I see also the trash and the junk, carelessly manufactured and carelessly thrown away, the glass and the broken glass and the plastic and the aluminum that will lie here longer than the lifetime of trees—longer than the lifetime of our species, perhaps. And I know that this also is what we have to show for our participation in the American economy, for most of the money made on these things too has been made elsewhere.

It would be somewhat more pleasant for country people if they could blame all this on city people. But the old opposition of country versus city—though still true, and truer than ever economically, for the country is more than ever the colony of the city—is far too simple to explain our problem. For country people more and more live like city people, and so connive in their own ruin. More and more country people, like city people, allow their economic and social standards to be set by television and salesmen and outside experts. Our garbage mingles with New Jersey garbage in our local landfill, and it would be hard to tell which is which.

As local community decays along with local economy, a vast amnesia settles over the countryside. As the exposed and disregarded soil departs with the rains, so local knowledge and local memory move away to the cities or are forgotten under the influence of homogenized sales talk, entertainment, and education. This loss of local knowledge and local memory—that is, of local culture—has been ignored, or written off as one of the cheaper "prices of progress," or made the business of folklorists. Nevertheless, local culture has a value, and part of its value is economic. This can be demonstrated readily enough.

For example, when a community loses its memory, its members no longer know one another. How can they know one another if they have forgotten or have never learned one another's stories? If they do not know one another's stories, how can they know whether or not to trust one another? People who do not trust one another do not help one another, and moreover they fear one another. And this is our predicament now. Because of a general distrust and suspicion, we not only lose one another's help and companionship, but we are all now living in jeopardy of being sued.

We don't trust our "public servants" because we know that they don't respect us. They don't respect us, as we understand, because they don't know us; they don't know our stories. They expect us to sue them if they make mistakes, and so they must insure themselves, at great expense to them and to us. Doctors in a country community must send their patients to specialists in the city, not necessarily because they believe that they are wrong in their diagnoses, but because they know that they are not infallible and they must protect themselves against lawsuits, at great expense to us.

The government of my home county, which has a population of about ten thousand people, pays an annual liability insurance premium of about $34,000. Add to this the liability premiums that are paid by every professional person who is "at risk" in the county, and you get some idea of the load we are carrying. Several decent family livelihoods are annually paid out of the county to insurance companies for a service that is only negative and provisional.

All of this money is lost to us by the failure of community. A good community, as we know, insures itself by trust, by good faith and good will, by mutual help. A good community, in other words, is a good local economy. It depends on itself for many of its essential needs and is thus shaped, so to speak, from the inside—unlike most modern populations that depend on distant purchases for almost everything and are thus shaped from the outside by the purposes and the influence of salesmen.

I was walking one Sunday afternoon several years ago with an older friend. We went by the ruining log house that had belonged to his grandparents and great-grandparents. The house stirred my friend's memory, and he told how the oldtime people used to visit each other in the evenings, especially in the long evenings of winter. There used to be a sort of institution in our part of the country known as "sitting till bedtime." After supper, when they weren't too tired, neighbors would walk across the fields to visit each other. They popped corn, my friend said, and ate apples and talked. They told each other stories. They told each other stories, as I knew myself, that they all had heard before. Sometimes they told stories about each other, about themselves, living again in their own memories and thus keeping their memories alive. Among the hearers of these stories were always the children. When bedtime came, the visitors lit their lanterns and went home. My friend talked about this, and thought about it, and then he said, "They had everything but money."

They were poor, as country people have often been, but they had each other, they had their local economy in which they helped each other, they had each other's comfort when they needed it, and they had their stories, their history together in that place. To have everything but money is to have much. And most people of the present can only marvel to think of neighbors entertaining themselves for a whole evening without a single imported pleasure and without listening to a single minute of sales talk.

Most of the descendants of those people have now moved away, partly because of the cultural and economic failures that I mentioned earlier, and most of them no longer sit in the evenings and talk to anyone. Most of them now sit until bedtime watching TV, submitting every few minutes to a sales talk. The message of both the TV programs and the sales talks is that the watchers should spend whatever is necessary to be like everybody else.

By television and other public means, we are encouraged to believe that we are far advanced beyond sitting till bedtime with the neighbors on a Kentucky ridgetop, and indeed beyond anything we ever were before. But if, for example, there should occur a forty-eight-hour power failure, we would find ourselves in much more backward circumstances than our ancestors. What, for starters, would we do for entertainment? Tell each other stories? But most of us no longer talk with each other, much less tell each other stories. We tell our stories now mostly to doctors or lawyers or psychiatrists or insurance adjusters or the police, not to our neighbors for their (and our) entertainment. The stories that now entertain us are made up for us in New York or Los Angeles or other centers of such commerce.

But a forty-eight-hour power failure would involve almost unimaginable deprivations. It would be difficult to travel, especially in cities. Most of the essential work could not be done. Our windowless modern schools and other such buildings that depend on air conditioning could not be used. Refrigeration would be impossible; food would spoil. It would be difficult or impossible to prepare meals. If it was winter, heating systems would fail. At the end of forty-eight hours many of us would be hungry.

Such a calamity (and it is a modest one among those that our time has made possible) would thus reveal how far most of us are now living from our cultural and economic sources, and how extensively we have destroyed the foundations of local life. It would show us how far we have strayed from the locally centered life of such neighborhoods as the one my friend described—a life based to a considerable extent on what we now call solar energy, which is decentralized, democratic, clean, and free. If we note that much of the difference we are talking about can be accounted for as an increasing dependence on energy sources that are centralized, undemocratic, filthy, and expensive, we will have completed a sort of historical parable.

How has this happened? There are many reasons for it. One of the chief reasons is that everywhere in our country the local succession of the generations has been broken. We can trace this change through a series of stories that we may think of as cultural landmarks.

Throughout most of our literature, the normal thing was for the generations to succeed one another in place. The memorable stories

occurred when this succession failed or became difficult or was somehow threatened. The norm is given in Psalm 128, in which this succession is seen as one of the rewards of righteousness: "Thou shalt see
thy children's children, and peace upon Israel."

The longing for this result seems to have been universal. It presides
also over *The Odyssey*, in which Odysseus' desire to return home is
certainly regarded as normal. And this story is also much concerned
with the psychology of family succession. Telemachus, Odysseus' son,
comes of age in preparing for the return of his long-absent father;
and it seems almost that Odysseus is enabled to return home by his
son's achievement of enough manhood to go in search of him. Long
after the return of both father and son, Odysseus' life will complete
itself, as we know from Teiresias' prophecy in Book XI, much in the
spirit of Psalm 128:

> *A seaborne death*
> *soft as this hand of mist will come upon you*
> *when you are wearied out with sick old age,*
> *your country folk in blessed peace around you.*

The Bible makes much of what it sees as the normal succession,
in such stories as those of Abraham, Isaac, and Jacob, or of David
and Solomon, in which the son completes the work or the destiny
of the father. The parable of the prodigal son is prepared for by such
Old Testament stories as that of Jacob, who errs, wanders, returns, is
forgiven, and takes his place in the family lineage.

Shakespeare was concerned throughout his working life with the
theme of the separation and rejoining of parents and children. It is
there at the beginning in *The Comedy of Errors*, and he is still thinking about it when he gets to *King Lear* and *Pericles* and *The Tempest*.
When Lear walks onstage with Cordelia dead in his arms, the theme
of return is fulfilled, only this time in the way of tragedy.

Wordsworth's poem "Michael," written in 1800, is in the same line

of descent. It is the story of a prodigal son, and return is still understood as the norm; before the boy's departure, he and his father make
a "covenant" that he will return home and carry on his father's life as
a shepherd on their ancestral pastures. But the ancient theme here
has two significant differences: The son leaves home for an economic
reason, and he does not return. Old Michael, the father, was long ago
"bound / In surety for his brother's son." This nephew has failed in
his business, and Michael is "summoned to discharge the forfeiture."
Rather than do this by selling a portion of their patrimony, the aged
parents decide that they must send their son to work for another
kinsman in the city in order to earn the necessary money. The country
people all are poor; there is no money to be earned at home. When
the son has cleared the debt from the land, he will return to it to "possess it, free as the wind / That passes over it." But the son goes to the
city, is corrupted by it, eventually commits a crime, and is forced "to
seek a hiding place beyond the seas."

"Michael" is a sort of cultural watershed. It carries on the theme
of return that goes back to the beginnings of Western culture, but
that return now is only a desire and a memory; in the poem it fails
to happen. Because of that failure, we see in "Michael" not just a
local story of the Lake District of England, which it is, but the story
of rural families in the industrial nations from Wordsworth's time
until today. The children go to the cities, for reasons imposed by the
external economy, and they do not return; eventually the parents die
and the family land, like Michael's, is sold to a stranger. By now it has
happened millions of times.

And by now the transformation of the ancient story is nearly
complete. Our society, on the whole, has forgotten or repudiated the
theme of return. Young people still grow up in rural families and go
off to the cities, not to return. But now it is felt that this is what they
should do. Now the norm is to leave and not return. And this applies as
much to urban families as to rural ones. In the present urban economy
the parent-child succession is possible only among the economically

privileged. The children of industrial underlings are not likely to succeed their parents at work, and there is no reason for them to wish
to do so. We are not going to have an industrial "Michael" in which
it is perceived as tragic that a son fails to succeed his father on an
assembly line.

According to the new norm, the child's destiny is not to succeed the parents, but to outmode them; succession has given way to
supersession. And this norm is institutionalized not in great communal stories, but in the education system. The schools are no longer
oriented to a cultural inheritance that it is their duty to pass on unim-
paired, but to the career, which is to say the future, of the child. The
orientation is thus necessarily theoretical, speculative, and merce-
nary. The child is not educated to return home and be of use to the
place and community; he or she is educated to *leave* home and earn
money in a provisional future that has nothing to do with place or
community. And parents with children in school are likely to find
themselves immediately separated from their children, and made
useless to them, by the intervention of new educational techniques,
technologies, methods, and languages. School systems innovate as
compulsively and as eagerly as factories. It is no wonder that, under
these circumstances, "educators" tend to look upon the parents as a
bad influence and wish to take the children away from home as early
as possible. And many parents, in truth, are now finding their children
an encumbrance at home, where there is no useful work for them to
do, and are glad enough to turn them over to the state for the use of
the future. The extent to which this order of things is now dominant
is suggested by a recent magazine article on the discovery of what
purports to be a new idea:

> The idea that a parent can be a teacher at home has caught the
> attention of educators. . . . Parents don't have to be graduates of
> Harvard or Yale to help their kids learn and achieve.[1]

Thus the home as a place where a child can learn becomes an *idea* of the professional "educator," who retains control of the idea. The home, as the article makes clear, is not to be a place where children may learn on their own, but a place where they are taught by parents according to the instructions of professional "educators." In fact, the Home and School Institute, Inc., of Washington, D.C., (known, of course, as "the HSI") has been "founded to show . . . how to involve families in their kids' educations."

In such ways as this, the nuclei of home and community have been invaded by the organizations, just as have the nuclei of cells and atoms. And we must be careful to see that the old cultural centers of home and community were made vulnerable to this invasion by their failure as economies. If there is no household or community economy, then family members and neighbors are no longer useful to one another. When people are no longer useful to one another, then the centripetal force of family and community fails, and people fall into dependence on exterior economies and organizations. The hegemony of professionals and professionalism erects itself on local failure, and from then on the locality exists merely as a market for consumer goods and as a source of "raw material," human and natural. The local schools no longer serve the local community; they serve the government's economy and the economy's government. Unlike the local community, the government and the economy cannot be served with affection, but only with professional zeal or professional boredom. Professionalism means more interest in salaries and less interest in what used to be known as disciplines. And so we arrive at the idea, endlessly reiterated in the news media, that education can be improved by bigger salaries for teachers—which may be true, but education cannot be improved, as the proponents too often imply, by bigger salaries alone. There must also be love of learning and of the cultural tradition and of excellence—and this love cannot exist, because it makes no sense, apart from the love of a place and a community.

Without this love, education is only the importation into a local community of centrally prescribed "career preparation" designed to facilitate the export of young careerists.

Our children are educated, then, to leave home, not to stay home, and the costs of this education have been far too little acknowledged. One of the costs is psychological, and the other is at once cultural and ecological.

The natural or normal course of human growing up must begin with some sort of rebellion against one's parents, for it is clearly impossible to grow up if one remains a child. But the child, in the process of rebellion and of achieving the emotional and economic independence that rebellion ought to lead to, finally comes to understand the parents as fellow humans and fellow sufferers, and in some manner returns to them as their friend, forgiven and forgiving the inevitable wrongs of family life. That is the old norm.

The new norm, according to which the child leaves home as a student and never lives at home again, interrupts the old course of coming of age at the point of rebellion, so that the child is apt to remain stalled in adolescence, never achieving any kind of reconciliation or friendship with the parents. Of course, such a return and reconciliation cannot be achieved without the recognition of mutual practical need. In the present economy, however, where individual dependences are so much exterior to both household and community, family members often have no practical need or use for one another. Hence the frequent futility of attempts at a purely psychological or emotional reconciliation.

And this interposition of rebellion and then of geographical and occupational distance between parents and children may account for the peculiar emotional intensity that our society attaches to innovation. We appear to hate whatever went before, very much as an adolescent hates parental rule, and to look on its obsolescence as a kind of vengeance. Thus we may explain industry's obsessive emphasis on "this year's model," or the preoccupation of the professional "educators" with theoretical and methodological innovation. Similarly, in modern literature we have had for many years an emphasis on "originality" and "the anxiety of influence" (an adolescent critical theory), as opposed, say, to Spenser's filial admiration for Chaucer, or Dante's for Virgil.

But if the new norm interrupts the development of the relation between children and parents, that same interruption, ramifying through a community, destroys the continuity and so the integrity of local life. As the children depart, generation after generation, the place loses its memory of itself, which is its history and its culture. And the local history, if it survives at all, loses its place. It does no good for historians, folklorists, and anthropologists to collect the songs and the stories and the lore that make up local culture and store them in books and archives. They cannot collect and store—because they cannot know—the pattern of reminding that can survive only in the living human community in its place. It is this pattern that is the life of local culture and that brings it usefully or pleasurably to mind. Apart from its local landmarks and occasions, the local culture may be the subject of curiosity or of study, but it is also dead.

The loss of local culture is, in part, a practical loss and an economic one. For one thing, such a culture contains, and conveys to succeeding generations, the history of the use of the place and the knowledge of how the place may be lived in and used. For another, the pattern of reminding implies affection for the place and respect for it, and so, finally, the local culture will carry the knowledge of how the place may be well and lovingly used, and also the implicit command to use it *only* well and lovingly. The only true and effective "operator's manual for spaceship earth" is not a book that any human will ever write; it is hundreds of thousands of local cultures.

Lacking an authentic local culture, a place is open to exploitation, and ultimately destruction, from the center. Recently, for example, I heard the dean of a prominent college of agriculture interviewed on the radio. What have we learned, he was asked, from last summer's drouth? And he replied that "we" need to breed more drouth resistance into plants, and that "we" need a government "safety net" for farmers. He might have said that farmers need to reexamine their farms and their circumstances in light of the drouth, and to think again on such subjects as diversification, scale, and the mutual helpfulness of neighbors. But he did not say that. To him, the drouth was merely an opportunity for agribusiness corporations and the government, by which the farmers and rural communities could only become more dependent on the economy that is destroying them. This is as good an example as any of the centralized thinking of a centralized economy—to which the only effective answer that I know is a strong local community with a strong local economy and a strong local culture.

For a long time now, the prevailing assumption has been that if the nation is all right, then all the localities within it will be all right also. I see little reason to believe that this is true. At present, in fact, both the nation and the national economy are living at the expense of localities and local communities—as all small-town and country people have reason to know. In rural America, which is in many ways a colony of what the government and the corporations think of as the nation, most of us have experienced the losses that I have been talking about: the departure of young people, of soil and other so-called natural resources, and of local memory. We feel ourselves crowded more and more into a dimensionless present, in which the past is forgotten and the future, even in our most optimistic "projections," is forbidding and fearful. Who can desire a future that is determined entirely by the purposes of the most wealthy and the most powerful, and by the capacities of machines?

Two questions, then, remain: Is a change for the better possible?

And who has the power to make such a change? I still believe that a change for the better is possible, but I confess that my belief is partly hope and partly faith. No one who hopes for improvement should fail to see and respect the signs that we may be approaching some sort of historical waterfall, past which we will not, by changing our minds, be able to change anything else. We know that at any time an ecological or a technological or a political event that we will have allowed may remove from us the power to make change and leave us with the mere necessity to submit to it. Beyond that, the two questions are one: The possibility of change depends on the existence of people who have the power to change.

Does this power reside at present in the national government? That seems to me extremely doubtful. To anyone who has read the papers during the recent presidential campaign, it must be clear that at the highest level of government there is, properly speaking, no political discussion. Are the corporations likely to help us? We know, from long experience, that the corporations will assume no responsibility that is not forcibly imposed upon them by government. The record of the corporations is written too plainly in verifiable damage to permit us to expect much from them. May we look for help to the universities? Well, the universities are more and more the servants of government and the corporations.

Most urban people evidently assume that all is well. They live too far from the exploited and endangered sources of their economy to need to assume otherwise. Some urban people are becoming disturbed about the contamination of air, water, and food, and that is promising, but there are not enough of them yet to make much difference. There is enough trouble in the "inner cities" to make them likely places of change, and evidently change is in them, but it is desperate and destructive change. As if to perfect their exploitation by other people, the people of the "inner cities" are destroying both themselves and their places.

My feeling is that if improvement is going to begin anywhere, it will have to begin out in the country and in the country towns. This is not because of any intrinsic virtue that can be ascribed to rural people, but because of their circumstances. Rural people are living, and have lived for a long time, at the site of the trouble. They see all around them, every day, the marks and scars of an exploitive national economy. They have much reason, by now, to know how little real help is to be expected from somewhere else. They still have, moreover, the remnants of local memory and local community. And in rural communities there are still farms and small businesses that can be changed according to the will and the desire of individual people.

In this difficult time of failed public expectations, when thoughtful people wonder where to look for hope, I keep returning in my own mind to the thought of the renewal of the rural communities. I know that one revived rural community would be more convincing and more encouraging than all the government and university programs of the last fifty years, and I think that it could be the beginning of the renewal of our country, for the renewal of rural communities ultimately implies the renewal of urban ones. But to be authentic, a true encouragement and a true beginning, this would have to be a revival accomplished mainly by the community itself. It would have to be done not from the outside by the instruction of visiting experts, but from the inside by the ancient rule of neighborliness, by the love of precious things, and by the wish to be at home.

(1988)

NOTE

1 Marianne Merrill Moates, "Learning … Every Day," *Creative Ideas for Living*, July/August 1988, p. 89.

Waste

∞

As a country person, I often feel that I am on the bottom end of the waste problem. I live on the Kentucky River about ten miles from its entrance into the Ohio. The Kentucky, in many ways a lovely river, receives an abundance of pollution from the Eastern Kentucky coal mines and the central Kentucky cities. When the river rises, it carries a continuous raft of cans, bottles, plastic jugs, chunks of styrofoam, and other imperishable trash. After the floods subside, I, like many other farmers, must pick up the trash before I can use my bottomland fields. I have seen the Ohio, whose name (*Oyo* in Iroquois) means "beautiful river," so choked with this manufactured filth that an ant could crawl dry-footed from Kentucky to Indiana. The air of both river valleys is seriously polluted. Our roadsides and roadside fields lie under a constant precipitation of cans, bottles, the plastic-ware of fast food joints, soiled plastic diapers, and sometimes whole bags of garbage. In our county we now have a "sanitary landfill" that daily receives, in addition to our local production, fifty to sixty large truck-loads of garbage from Pennsylvania, New Jersey, and New York.

Moreover, a close inspection of our countryside would reveal, strewn over it from one end to the other, thousands of derelict and worthless automobiles, house trailers, refrigerators, stoves, freezers, washing machines, and dryers; as well as thousands of unregulated dumps in hollows and sink holes, on streambanks and roadsides, filled not only with "disposable" containers but also with broken toasters, television sets, toys of all kinds, furniture, lamps, stereos, radios, scales, coffee makers, mixers, blenders, corn poppers, hair dryers, and micro-wave ovens. Much of our waste problem is to be accounted for by the intentional flimsiness and unrepairability of the labor-savers and gadgets that we have become addicted to.

Of course, my sometime impression that I live on the receiving end of this problem is false, for country people contribute their full share. The truth is that we Americans, all of us, have become a kind of human trash, living our lives in the midst of a ubiquitous damned mess of which we are at once the victims and the perpetrators. We are all unwilling victims, perhaps; and some of us even are unwilling perpetrators, but we must count ourselves among the guilty none-theless. In my household we produce much of our own food and try to do without as many frivolous "necessities" as possible—and yet, like everyone else, we must shop, and when we shop we must bring home a load of plastic, aluminum, and glass containers designed to be thrown away, and "appliances" designed to wear out quickly and be thrown away.

I confess that I am angry at the manufacturers who make these things. There are days when I would be delighted if certain corpora-tion executives could somehow be obliged to eat their products. I know of no good reason why these containers and all other forms of manufactured "waste"—solid, liquid, toxic, or whatever—should not be outlawed. There is no sense and no sanity in objecting to the desecration of the flag while tolerating and justifying and encouraging as a daily business the desecration of the country for which it stands.

But our waste problem is not the fault only of producers. It is the fault of an economy that is wasteful from top to bottom—a symbiosis of an unlimited greed at the top and a lazy, passive, and self-indulgent consumptiveness at the bottom—and all of us are involved in it. If we wish to correct this economy, we must be careful to understand and to demonstrate how much waste of human life is involved in our waste of the material goods of Creation. For example, much of the litter that now defaces our country is fairly directly caused by the massive secession or exclusion of most of our people from active participation in the food economy. We have made a social ideal of minimal involvement in the growing and cooking of food. This is one of the dearest "liberations" of our affluence. Nevertheless, the more dependent we become on the *industries* of eating and drinking, the more waste we are going to produce. The mess that surrounds us, then, must be understood not just as a problem in itself but as a symptom of a greater and graver problem: the centralization of our economy, the gathering of the productive property and power into fewer and fewer hands, and the consequent destruction, everywhere, of the local economies of household, neighborhood, and community.

This is the source of our unemployment problem, and I am not talking just about the unemployment of eligible members of the "labor force." I mean also the unemployment of children and old people, who, in viable household and local economies, would have work to do by which they would be useful to themselves and to others. The ecological damage of centralization and waste is thus inextricably involved with human damage. For we have, as a result, not only a desecrated, ugly, and dangerous country in which to live until we are in some manner poisoned by it, and a constant and now generally accepted problem of unemployed or unemployable workers, but also classrooms full of children who lack the experience and discipline of fundamental human tasks, and various institutions full of still capable old people who are useless and lonely.

I think that we must learn to see the trash on our streets and road-sides, in our rivers, and in our woods and fields, not as the side effect of "more jobs" as its manufacturers invariably insist that it is, but as evidence of good work *not* done by people able to do it.

(1989)

Conserving Forest Communities*

∞

I live in Henry County, near the lower end of the Kentucky River Valley, on a small farm that is half woodland. Starting from my back door, I could walk for days and never leave the woods except to cross the roads. Though Henry County is known as a farming county, 25 percent of it is wooded. From the hillside behind my house I can see thousands of acres of trees in the counties of Henry, Owen, and Carroll.

Most of the trees are standing on steep slopes of the river and creek valleys that were cleared and plowed at intervals from the early years of settlement until about the time of World War II. These are rich woodlands nevertheless. The soil, though not so deep as it once was,

* Delivered as a speech at the Kentucky Forest Summit (in conjunction with the Nineteenth Governor's Conference on the Environment) at Louisville, Kentucky, September 29, 1994.

is healing from agricultural abuse and, because of the forest cover, is increasing in fertility. The plant communities consist of some cedar and a great diversity of hardwoods, shrubs, and wild flowers.

The history of these now-forested slopes over the last two centuries can be characterized as a cyclic alternation of abuse and neglect. Their best hope, so far, has been neglect—though even neglect has often involved their degradation by livestock grazing. So far, almost nobody has tried to figure out or has even wondered what might be the best use and the best care for such places. Often the trees have been regarded merely as obstructions to row-cropping, which, because of the steepness of the terrain, has necessarily caused severe soil losses from water erosion. If an accounting is ever done, we will be shocked to learn how much ecological capital this kind of farming required for an almost negligible economic return: Thousands of years of soil building were squandered on a few crops of corn or tobacco.

In my part of Kentucky, as in other parts, we never developed a local forest economy, and I think this was because of our preoccupation with tobacco. In the wintertime when farmers in New England, for example, employed themselves in the woods, our people went to their stripping rooms. Though in the earliest times we depended on the maple groves for syrup and sugar, we did not do so for very long. In this century, the fossil fuels weaned most of our households from firewood. For those reasons and others, we have never very consistently or very competently regarded trees as an economic resource.

And so as I look at my home landscape, I am happy to see that I am to a considerable extent a forest dweller. But I am unhappy to remember every time I look—for the landscape itself reminds me-that I am a dweller in a forest for which there is, properly speaking, no local forest culture and no local forest economy. That is to say that I live in a threatened forest.

Such woodlands as I have been describing are now mostly ignored so long as they are young. After the trees have reached marketable size, especially in a time of agricultural depression, the landowners come under pressure to sell them. And then the old cycle is repeated, as neglect is once more superseded by abuse. The salable trees are marked, and the tract of timber is sold to somebody who may have no connection, economic or otherwise, to the local community. The trees are likely to be felled and dragged from the woods in ways that do more damage than necessary to the land and the young trees. The skidder may take the logs straight upslope, leaving scars that (depending on how they catch the runoff) will be slow to heal or will turn into gullies that will never heal. There is no local *interest* connecting the woods workers to the woods. They do not regard the forest as a permanent resource but rather as a purchased "crop" that must be "harvested" as quickly and as cheaply as possible.

The economy of this kind of forestry is apt to be as deplorable as its ecology. More than likely only the prime log of each tree is taken— that is, the felled tree is cut in two below the first sizable branch, leaving many board feet in short logs (that would be readily usable, say, if there were small local woodworking shops) as well as many cords of firewood. The trees thus carelessly harvested will most likely leave the local community and the state as sawlogs or, at best, rough lumber. The only local economic benefit may well be the single check paid by the timber company to the landowner.

But the small landowners themselves may not receive the optimum benefit, for the prevailing assumptions and economic conditions encourage or require them to sell all their marketable trees at the same time. Unless the landowner is also a logger with the know-how and the means of cutting timber and removing it from the woods, the small, privately owned woodland is not likely to be considered a source of steady income, producing a few trees every year or every few years. For most such landowners in Kentucky, a timber sale may be thinkable only once or twice in a lifetime.

Furthermore, such landowners now must, as a matter of course, sell their timber on a market in which they have no influence, in which the power is held almost exclusively by the buyer. The sellers, of course, may choose not to sell—but only if they can *afford* not to sell. The private owners of Kentucky woodlands are in much the same fix that Kentucky tobacco producers were in before the time of the Burley Tobacco Growers Cooperative Association—and in much the same fix as most American farmers today. They cannot go to market except by putting themselves at the mercy of the market. This is a matter of no little significance and concern in a rural state in which 90.9 percent of the forestland "is owned by approximately 440,000 nonindustrial private owners, whose average holding is 26 acres." [1]

I have been describing one version of present-day commercial forestry in Kentucky—what might be called the casual version.

But we also have in view another version. This is the big-money, large-scale corporate version. It involves the building of a large factory in a forested region, predictably accompanied by political advertisements about "job creation" and "improving the local economy." This factory, instead of sawing trees into boards, will reduce them to pulp for making paper, or it will grind or shred them and make boards or prefabricated architectural components by gluing together the resulting chips or strands.

Obviously, there are some advantages to these methods. Pulping or shredding can certainly use more of a tree than, say, a conventional sawmill. The laminated-strand process can make good building material out of low-quality trees. And there is no denying our society's need for paper and for building materials.

But from the point of view of either the forest or the local human community, there are also a number of problems associated with this kind of operation.

The fundamental problem is that it is costly and large in scale. It is therefore beyond the reach of small rural communities and so will be run inevitably for the benefit not of the local people but of absentee investors. And because of its cost and size, a large wood products factory establishes in the local forest an enormous appetite for trees.

The very efficiency of a shredding mill—its ability to use small or low-quality trees—necessarily predisposes it to clear-cutting rather than to selective and sustained production. And a well-known inclination of such industries is toward forest monocultures, which do not have the ecological stability of natural forests.

As Kentuckians know from plenty of experience, nonexploitive relationships between large industries and small communities are extremely rare, if they exist at all. A large industrial operation might conceivably be established upon the most generous and forbearing principles of forestry and with the most benevolent intentions toward the local people. But we must remember that this large operation involves a large investment. And experience has taught us that large investments tend to take precedence over ecosystems and communities. In a time of economic adversity, the community and the forest will be sacrificed before the factory will be. The ideal of such operations is maximum profit to the owners or shareholders, who are not likely to be members of the local community. This means what it has always meant: Labor and materials must be procured as cheaply as possible, and real human and ecological costs must be "externalized"— charged to taxpayers or to the future.

And so Kentucky forestry, at present, is mainly of two kinds: the casual and careless logging that is hardly more than an afterthought of farming, and the large-scale exploitation of the forest by absentee owners of corporations. Neither kind is satisfactory, by any responsible measure, in a state whose major natural resources will always be its productive soils and whose landscape today is one-half forested.

Kentucky has 12,700,000 acres of forest—almost 20,000 square miles. Very little of this is mature forest; nearly all of the old-growth timber had been cut down by 1940. Kentucky woodlands are nevertheless a valuable economic resource, supporting at present a wood-products industry with an annual payroll of $300 million and employing about 25,000 people. In addition, our forestlands contribute significantly to Kentucky's attractiveness to tourists, hunters, fishermen, and campers. They contribute indirectly to the economy by protecting our watersheds and our health.

But however valuable our forests may be now, they are nothing like so valuable as they can become. If we use the young forests we have now in the best way and if we properly care for them, they will continue to increase in board footage, in health, and in beauty for several more human generations. But already we are running into problems that can severely limit the value and usefulness of this resource to our people, because we have neglected to learn to practice good forest stewardship.

Moreover, we have never understood that the only appropriate human response to a diversified forest ecosystem is a diversified local forest economy. We have failed so far to imagine and put in place the sort of small-scale, locally owned logging and wood-products industries that would be the best guarantors of the long-term good use and good care of our forests. At present, it is estimated that up to 70 percent of the timber production of our forests leaves the state as logs or as raw lumber.

Lest you think that the situation and the problems I have outlined are of interest only to "tree huggers," let me remind you that during most of the history of our state, our rural landscapes and our rural communities have been in bondage to an economic colonialism that has exploited and misused both land and people. This exploitation has tended to become more severe with the growth of industrial technology. It has been most severe and most obvious in the coalfields of eastern Kentucky, but it has been felt and has produced its dire effects everywhere. With few exceptions our country people, generation after generation, have been providers of cheap fuels and raw materials to be used or manufactured in other places and to the profit of other people. They have added no value to what they have produced, and they have gone onto the markets without protection. They have sold their labor, their mineral rights, their crops, their livestock, and their trees with the understanding that the offered price was the price that they must take. Except for the tobacco program and the coal miners' union, rural Kentuckians have generally been a people without an asking price. We have developed the psychology of a subject people, willing to take whatever we have been offered and to believe whatever we have been told by our self-designated "superiors."

Now, with the two staple economies of coal and tobacco in doubt, we ask, "What can we turn to?" This is a question for every Kentuckian, but immediately it is a question for the rural communities. It is a question we may have to hold before ourselves for a long time, because the answer is going to be complex and difficult. If, however, as a part of the answer, we say, "Timber," I believe we will be right.

But we must be careful. In the past we have too often merely trusted that the corporate economy or the government would dispose of natural resources in a way that would be best for the land and the people. I hope we will not do that again. That trust has too often been catastrophically misplaced. From now on we should disbelieve that any corporation ever comes to any rural place to do it good, to "create jobs," or to bring to the local people the benefits of the so-called free market. It will be a tragedy if the members of Kentucky's rural communities ever again allow themselves passively to be sold off as providers of cheap goods and cheap labor. To put the bounty and the health of our land, our only commonwealth, into the hands of people who do not live on it and share its fate will always be an error. For whatever determines the fortune of the land determines also the fortune of the people. If the history of Kentucky teaches anything, it teaches that.

But the peculiarity of our history, so far, is that we have not had to learn the lesson. When the Old World races settled here, they saw a natural abundance so vast they could not imagine that it could be exhausted or ruined. Because it was vast and because virtually a whole continent was opening to the west, many of our forebears felt free to use the land carelessly and to justify their carelessness on the assumption that they could escape what they ruined. That early regardlessness of consequence infected our character, and so far it has dominated the political and economic life of our state. So far, for every Kentuckian, like Harry Caudill, willing to speak of the natural limits within which we have been living all along, there have been many who have wished only to fill their pockets and move on, leaving their ecological debts to be paid by somebody else's children.

But by this time, the era of cut-and-run economics *ought* to be finished. Such an economy cannot be rationally defended or even apologized for. The proofs of its immense folly, heartlessness, and destructiveness are everywhere. Its failure as a way of dealing with the natural world and human society can no longer be sanely denied. That this economic system persists and grows larger and stronger in spite of its evident failure has nothing to do with rationality or, for that matter, with evidence. It persists because, embodied now in multinational corporations, it has discovered a terrifying truth: If you can control a people's economy, you don't need to worry about its politics; its politics have become irrelevant. If you control people's choices as to whether or not they will work, and where they will work, and what they will do, and how well they will do it, and what they will eat and wear, and the genetic makeup of their crops and animals, and what they will do for amusement, then why should you worry about freedom of speech? In a totalitarian economy, any "political liberties" that the people might retain would simply cease to matter. If, as is often the case already, nobody can be elected who is not wealthy, and if nobody can be wealthy without dependence on the corporate economy, then what is your vote worth? The citizen thus becomes an economic subject.

A totalitarian economy might "correct" itself, of course, by a total catastrophe—total explosion or total contamination or total ecological exhaustion. A far better correction, however, would be a cumulative process by which states, regions, communities, households, or even individuals would begin to work toward economic self-determination and an appropriate measure of local independence. Such a course of action would involve us in a renewal of thought about our history and our predicament. We must ask again whether or not we really want to be a free people. We must consider again the linkages between land and landownership and land use and liberty. And we must ask, as we have not very seriously asked before, what are the best ways to use and to care for our land, our neighbors, and our natural resources.

If economists ever pay attention to such matters, they may find that as the scale of an enterprise increases, its standards become more and more simple, and it answers fewer and fewer needs in the local community. For example, in the summer of 1982, according to an article in *California Forestry Notes*, three men, using five horses, removed 400,780 board feet from a 35.5-acre tract in Latour State Forest.[2] This was a "thinning operation." Two of the men worked full time as teamsters, using two horses each; one man felled the trees and did some skidding with a single horse. The job required sixty-four days. It was profitable both for the state forest and for the operator. During the sixty-four days the skidders barked a total of eight trees, only one of which was damaged badly enough to require removal. Soil disturbance in the course of the operation was rated as "slight."

At the end of this article the author estimates that a tractor could have removed the logs two and a half times as fast as the horses. And thus he implies a question that he does not attempt to answer: Is it better for two men and four horses to work sixty-four days, or for one man and one machine to do the same work in twenty-five and a half days? Assuming that the workers would all be from the local community, it is clear that the community, a timber company, and a manufacturer of mechanical skidders would answer that question in different ways. The timber company and the manufacturer would answer on the basis of a purely economic efficiency: the need to produce the greatest volume, hence the greatest profit, in the shortest time. The community, on the contrary—and just as much as a matter of self-interest—might reasonably prefer the way of working that employed the most people for the longest time and did the least damage to the forest and the soil. The community might conclude that the machine, in addition to the ecological costs of its manufacture and use, not only replaced the work of one man but more than halved the working time of another. From the point of view of the community, it is *not* an improvement when the number of employed workers is reduced by the introduction of labor-saving machinery.

This question of which technology is better is one that our society has almost never thought to ask on behalf of the local community. It is clear nevertheless that the corporate standard of judgment, in this instance as in others, is radically oversimplified, and that the community standard is sufficiently complex. By using more people to do better work, the economic need is met, but so are other needs that are social and ecological, cultural and religious.

We can safely predict that for a long time there are going to be people in places of power who will want to solve our local problems by inviting in some great multinational corporation. They will want to put millions of dollars of public money into an "incentive package" to make it worthwhile for the corporation to pay low wages for our labor and to pay low prices for, let us say, our timber. It is well understood that nothing so excites the glands of a free-market capitalist as the offer of a government subsidy.

But before we agree again to so radical a measure, producing maximum profits to people who live elsewhere and minimal, expensive benefits to ourselves and our neighbors, we ought to ask if we cannot contrive local solutions for our local problems, and if the local solutions might not be the best ones. It is not enough merely to argue against a renewal of the old colonial economy. We must have something else competently in mind.

If we don't want to subject our forests to the rule of absentee exploiters, then we must ask what kind of forest economy we would like to have. By "we" I mean all the people of our state, of course, but I mean also, and especially, the people of our state's rural counties and towns and neighborhoods.

Obviously, I cannot speak for anybody but myself. But as a citizen of this state and a member of one of its rural communities, I would like to offer a description of what I believe would be a good forest economy. The following are not my own ideas, as you will see, but come from the work of many people who have put first in their thoughts the survival and the good health of their communities.

A good forest economy, like any other good land-based economy, would aim to join the local human community and the local natural community or ecosystem together as conservingly and as healthfully as possible.

A good forest economy would therefore be a local economy, and the forest economy of a state or region would therefore be a decentralized economy. The only reason to centralize such an economy is to concentrate its profits into the fewest hands. A good forest economy would be owned locally. It would afford a decent livelihood to local people. And it would propose to serve local needs and fill local demands first, before seeking markets elsewhere.

A good forest economy would preserve the local forest in its native diversity, quality, health, abundance, and beauty. It would recognize no distinction between its own prosperity and the prosperity of the forest ecosystem. A good forest economy would function in part as a sort of lobby for the good use of the forest.

A good forest economy would be properly scaled. Individual

enterprises would be no bigger than necessary to ensure the best work and the best livelihood for workers. The ruling purpose would be to do the work with the least possible disturbance to the local ecosystem and the local human community. Keeping the scale reasonably small is good for the forest. Only a local, small-scale forest economy would permit, for example, the timely and selective logging of small woodlots. Another benefit of smallness of scale is that it preserves economic democracy and the right of private property. Property boundaries, as we should always remember, are human conventions, useful for defining not only privileges but also responsibilities, so that use may always be accompanied by knowledge, affection, care, and skill. Such boundaries exist only because the society as a whole agrees to their existence. If the right of landownership is used only to protect an owner's wish to abuse or destroy the land, upon which the community's welfare ultimately depends, then society's interest in maintaining the convention understandably declines. And so in the interest of democracy and property rights, there is much to be gained by keeping especially the land-based industries small.

A good forest economy would be locally complex. People in the local community would be employed in forest management, logging, and sawmilling, in a variety of value-adding small factories and shops, and in satellite or supporting industries. The local community, that is, would be enabled by its economy to realize the maximum income from its local resource. This is the opposite of a colonial economy. It would answer unequivocally the question, To *whom* is the value added?

Furthermore, a local forest economy, living by the measure of local economic health, might be led to some surprising alterations of logging technology. For example, it would almost certainly have to look again at the use of draft animals in logging. This would not only be kinder to the forest but would also be another way of elaborating the economy locally, requiring lower investment and less spending outside the community.

A good forest economy would make good forestry attractive to landowners, providing income from recreational uses of their woodlands, markets for forest products other than timber, and so on.

A good forest economy would obviously need to be much interested in local education. It would, of course, need to pass on to its children the large culture's inheritance of book learning. But also, both at home and in school, it would want its children to acquire a competent knowledge of local geography, ecology, history, natural history, and of local songs and stories. And it would want a system of apprenticeships, constantly preparing young people to carry on the local work in the best way.

All along, I have been implying that a good forest economy would be a limited economy. It would be limited in scale and limited by the several things it would not do. But it would be limited also by the necessity to leave some wilderness tracts of significant acreage unused. Because of its inclination to be proud and greedy, human character needs this practical deference toward things greater than itself; this is, I think, a religious deference. Also, for reasons of self-interest and our own survival, we need wilderness as a standard. Wilderness gives us the indispensable pattern and measure of sustainability.

To assure myself that what I have described as a good forest economy is a real possibility, I went to visit the tribal forest of the Menominee Indians in northern Wisconsin. In closing, I want to say what I learned about that forest—from reading; from talking with Marshall Pecore, the forest manager, and others; and from seeing for myself.

The Menominee originally inhabited a territory of perhaps ten million acres in Wisconsin and northern Michigan. By the middle of the nineteenth century, as the country was taken up by white settlers, the tribal holding had been reduced to 235,000 acres, 220,000 acres of which were forested.

The leaders understood that if the Menominee were to live, they would have to give up their old life of hunting and gathering and make timber from their forest a major staple of their livelihood; they understood also that if the Menominee were to survive as a people, they would have to preserve the forest while they lived from it. And so in 1854 they started logging, having first instituted measures to ensure that neither the original nature nor the productive capacity of the forest would be destroyed by their work. Now, 140 years later, Menominee forest management has become technically sophisticated, but it is still rooted in cultural tradition, and its goal has remained exactly the same: to preserve the identification of the human community with the forest, and to give an absolute priority to the forest's ecological integrity. The result, in comparison to the all-too-common results of land use in the United States, is astonishing. In 1854, when logging was begun, the forest contained an estimated billion and a half board feet of standing timber. No records exist for the first thirteen years, but from 1865 to 1988 the forest yielded two billion board feet. And today, after 140 years of continuous logging, the forest still is believed to contain a billion and a half board feet of standing timber. Over those 140 years, the average diameter of the trees has been reduced by only one half of one inch—and that by design, for the foresters want fewer large hemlocks.

About 20 percent of the forest is managed in even-aged stands of aspen and jack pine, which are harvested by clear-cutting and which regenerate naturally. The rest of the forest is divided into 109 compartments, to each of which the foresters return every fifteen years to select trees for cutting. Their rule is to cut the worst and leave the best. That is, the loggers remove only those trees that are unlikely to survive for another fifteen years, those that are stunted or otherwise defective, and those that need to be removed in order to improve the stand. Old trees that are healthy and still growing are left uncut. As a result, this is an old forest, containing, for example, 350-year-old hemlocks, as well as cedars that are probably older. The average age of harvested maples is 140 to 180 years.

In support of this highly selective cutting, the forest is kept under constant study and evaluation. And loggers in the forest are strictly regulated and supervised. Even though the topography of the forest is comparatively level, skidders must be small and rubber-tired. Loggers must use permanent skid trails. And all logging contractors must attend training sessions.

The Menominee forest economy currently employs—in forest management, logging, milling, and other work—215 tribe members, or nearly 16 percent of the adult population of the reservation. As the Menominee themselves know, this is not enough; the economy of the forest needs to be more diverse. Its products at present are sawed lumber, logs, veneer logs, pulpwood, and "specialty woods" such as paneling and moldings. More value-adding industries are needed, and the Menominee are working on the problem. One knowledgeable observer has estimated that "they could probably turn twice the profit with half the land under management if they used more secondary processing."[3]

Kentuckians looking for the pattern of a good local forest economy would have to conclude, I think, that the Menominee example is not complex enough, but that in all other ways it is excellent. We have much to learn from it. The paramount lesson undoubtedly is that the Menominee forest economy is as successful as it is because it is not understood primarily as an economy. Everybody I talked to on my visit urged me to understand that the forest is the basis of a culture and that the unrelenting cultural imperative has been to keep the forest intact—to preserve its productivity and the diversity of its trees, both in species and in age. The goal has always been a diverse, old, healthy, beautiful, productive, community-supporting forest that is home not only to its wild inhabitants but also to its human community. To secure this goal, the Menominee, following the dictates of their culture, have always done their work bearing in mind the needs of the seventh generation of their descendants.

And so, to complete my description of a good forest economy, I

must add that it would be a long-term economy. Our modern economy is still essentially a crop-year economy—as though industrialism
had founded itself upon the principles of the worst sort of agriculture.
The ideal of the industrial economy is to shorten as much as possible
the interval separating investment and payoff; it wants to make things
fast, especially money. But even the slightest acquaintance with the
vital statistics of trees places us in another kind of world. A forest
makes things slowly; a good forest economy would therefore be a
patient economy. It would also be an unselfish one, for good foresters
must always look toward harvests that they will not live to reap.

(1994)

NOTES

1 William H. Martin, Mark Matuszewski, Robert N. Muller, and Bradley E.
Powell, "Kentucky's Forest Resources" (unpublished paper), 3. I have taken sta-
tistics and other information on Kentucky forests from this paper and also from
William H. Martin, "Sustainable Forestry in Kentucky," *In Context* (Center for
Economic Development at Eastern Kentucky University, winter 1993), 1, 5-6;
and William H. Martin, "Characteristics of Old Growth Mixed Mesophytic
Forests," *Natural Areas Journal* 12, no. 3 (July 1992): 127-135.

2 Dave McNamara, "Horse Logging at Latour," *California Forestry Notes* (Sept.
1983): 1-10.

3 Scott Landis, "Seventh-Generation Forestry," *Harrowsmith Country Life* (Nov./
Dec. 1992): 33. I also made use of Marshall Pecore, "Menominee Sustained-Yield
Management," *Journal of Forestry* (July 1992): 12-16.

The Total Economy

∞

Let us begin by assuming what appears to be true: that the so-called environmental crisis is now pretty well established as a fact of our age. The problems of pollution, species extinction, loss of wilderness, loss of farmland, and loss of topsoil may still be ignored or scoffed at, but they are not denied. Concern for these problems has acquired a certain standing, a measure of discussability, in the media and in some scientific, academic, and religious institutions.

This is good, of course; obviously, we can't hope to solve these problems without an increase of public awareness and concern. But in an age burdened with "publicity," we have to be aware also that as issues rise into popularity they rise also into the danger of oversimplification. To speak of this danger is especially necessary in confronting the destructiveness of our relationship to nature, which is the result, in the first place, of gross oversimplification.

The "environmental crisis" has happened because the human household or economy is in conflict at almost every point with the household of nature. We have built our household on the assumption that the natural household is simple and can be simply used. We have assumed increasingly over the last five hundred years that nature is merely a supply of "raw materials," and that we may safely possess those materials merely by taking them. This taking, as our technical means have increased, has involved always less reverence or respect, less gratitude, less local knowledge, and less skill. Our methodologies of land use have strayed from our old sympathetic attempts to imitate natural processes, and have come more and more to resemble the methodology of mining, even as mining itself has become more powerful technologically and more brutal.

And so we will be wrong if we attempt to correct what we perceive as "environmental" problems without correcting the economic oversimplification that caused them. This oversimplification is now either a matter of corporate behavior or of behavior under the influence of corporate behavior. This is sufficiently clear to many of us. What is not sufficiently clear, perhaps to any of us, is the extent of our complicity, as individuals and especially as individual consumers, in the behavior of the corporations.

What has happened is that most people in our country, and apparently most people in the "developed" world, have given proxies to the corporations to produce and provide *all of* their food, clothing, and shelter. Moreover, they are rapidly increasing their proxies to corporations or governments to provide entertainment, education, child care, care of the sick and the elderly, and many other kinds of "service" that once were carried on informally and inexpensively by individuals or households or communities. Our major economic practice, in short, is to delegate the practice to others.

The danger now is that those who are concerned will believe that the solution to the "environmental crisis" can be merely political—

that the problems, being large, can be solved by large solutions generated by a few people to whom we will give our proxies to police the economic proxies that we have already given. The danger, in other words, is that people will think they have made a sufficient change if they have altered their "values," or had a "change of heart," or experienced a "spiritual awakening," and that such a change in passive consumers will necessarily cause appropriate changes in the public experts, politicians, and corporate executives to whom they have granted their political and economic proxies.

The trouble with this is that a proper concern for nature and our use of nature must be practiced, not by our proxy-holders, but by ourselves. A change of heart or of values without a practice is only another pointless luxury of a passively consumptive way of life. The "environmental crisis," in fact, can be solved only if people, individually and in their communities, recover responsibility for their thoughtlessly given proxies. If people begin the effort to take back into their own power a significant portion of their economic responsibility, then their inevitable first discovery is that the "environmental crisis" is no such thing; it is not a crisis of our environs or surroundings; it is a crisis of our lives as individuals, as family members, as community members, and as citizens. We have an "environmental crisis" because *we* have consented to an economy in which by eating, drinking, working, resting, traveling, and enjoying ourselves we are destroying the natural, the God-given, world.

We live, as we must sooner or later recognize, in an era of sentimental economics and, consequently, of sentimental politics. Sentimental communism holds in effect that everybody and everything should suffer for the good of "the many" who, though miserable in the present, will be happy in the future for exactly the same reasons that they are miserable in the present.

Sentimental capitalism is not so different from sentimental

communism as the corporate and political powers claim to suppose. Sentimental capitalism holds in effect that everything small, local, private, personal, natural, good, and beautiful must be sacrificed in the interest of the "free market" and the great corporations, which will bring unprecedented security and happiness to "the many"—in, of course, the future.

These forms of political economy may be described as sentimental because they depend absolutely upon a political faith for which there is no justification. They seek to preserve the gullibility of the people by issuing a cold check on a fund of political virtue that does not exist. Communism and "free-market" capitalism both are modern versions of oligarchy. In their propaganda, both justify violent means by good ends, which always are put beyond reach by the violence of the means. The trick is to define the end vaguely—"the greatest good of the greatest number" or "the benefit of the many"—and keep it at a distance. For example, the United States government's agricultural policy, or nonpolicy, since 1952 has merely consented to the farmers' predicament of high costs and low prices; it has never envisioned or advocated in particular the prosperity of farmers or of farmland, but has only promised "cheap food" to consumers and "survival" to the "larger and more efficient" farmers who supposedly could adapt to and endure the attrition of high costs and low prices. And after each inevitable wave of farm failures and the inevitable enlargement of the destitution and degradation of the countryside, there have been the inevitable reassurances from government propagandists and university experts that American agriculture was now more efficient and that everybody would be better off in the future.

The fraudulence of these oligarchic forms of economy is in their principle of displacing whatever good they recognize (as well as their debts) from the present to the future. Their success depends upon persuading people, first, that whatever they have now is no good, and, second, that the promised good is certain to be achieved in the future.

This obviously contradicts the principle—common, I believe, to all the religious traditions—that if ever we are going to do good to one another, then the time to do it is now; we are to receive no reward for promising to do it in the future. And both communism and capitalism have found such principles to be a great embarrassment. If you are presently occupied in destroying every good thing in sight in order to do good in the future, it is inconvenient to have people saying things like "Love thy neighbor as thyself" or "Sentient beings are numberless, I vow to save them." Communists and capitalists alike, "liberal" capitalists and "conservative" capitalists alike, have needed to replace religion with some form of determinism, so that they can say to their victims, "I'm doing this because I can't do otherwise. It is not my fault. It is inevitable." This is a lie, obviously, and religious organizations have too often consented to it.

The idea of an economy based upon several kinds of ruin may seem a contradiction in terms, but in fact such an economy is possible, as we see. It is possible, however, on one implacable condition: The only future good that it assuredly leads to is that it will destroy itself. And how does it disguise this outcome from its subjects, its short-term beneficiaries, and its victims? It does so by false accounting. It substitutes for the real economy, by which we build and maintain (or do not maintain) our household, a symbolic economy of money, which in the long run, because of the self-interested manipulations of the "controlling interests," cannot symbolize or account for anything but itself. And so we have before us the spectacle of unprecedented "prosperity" and "economic growth" in a land of degraded farms, forests, ecosystems, and watersheds, polluted air, failing families, and perishing communities.

This moral and economic absurdity exists for the sake of the allegedly "free" market, the single principle of which is this: Commodities will be produced wherever they can be produced at the lowest cost and consumed wherever they will bring the highest price. To make too cheap and sell too high has always been the program of industrial capitalism. The global "free market" is merely capitalism's so far successful attempt to enlarge the geographic scope of its greed, and moreover to give to its greed the status of a "right" within its presumptive territory. The global "free market" is free to the corporations precisely because it dissolves the boundaries of the old national colonialisms, and replaces them with a new colonialism without restraints or boundaries. It is pretty much as if all the rabbits have now been forbidden to have holes, thereby "freeing" the hounds.

The "right" of a corporation to exercise its economic power without restraint is construed, by the partisans of the "free market," as a form of freedom, a political liberty implied presumably by the right of individual citizens to own and use property.

But the "free market" idea introduces into government a sanction of an inequality that is not implicit in any idea of democratic liberty: namely that the "free market" is freest to those who have the most money, and is not free at all to those with little or no money. Wal-Mart, for example, as a large corporation "freely" competing against local, privately owned businesses, has virtually all the freedom, and its small competitors virtually none.

To make too cheap and sell too high, there are two requirements. One is that you must have a lot of consumers with surplus money and unlimited wants. For the time being, there are plenty of these consumers in the "developed" countries. The problem, for the time being easily solved, is simply to keep them relatively affluent and dependent on purchased supplies.

The other requirement is that the market for labor and raw materials should remain depressed relative to the market for retail commodities. This means that the supply of workers should exceed demand, and that the land-using economies should be allowed or encouraged to overproduce.

To keep the cost of labor low, it is necessary first to entice or force country people everywhere in the world to move into the cities—in the manner prescribed by the Committee for Economic Development after World War II—and, second, to continue to introduce labor-replacing technology. In this way it is possible to maintain a "pool" of people who are in the threatful position of being mere consumers, landless and poor, and who therefore are eager to go to work for low wages—precisely the condition of migrant farm workers in the United States.

To cause the land-using economies to overproduce is even simpler. The farmers and other workers in the world's land-using economies, by and large, are not organized. They are therefore unable to control production in order to secure just prices. Individual producers must go individually to the market and take for their produce simply whatever they are paid. They have no power to bargain or to make demands. Increasingly, they must sell, not to neighbors or to neighboring towns and cities, but to large and remote corporations. There is no competition among the buyers (supposing there is more than one), who *are* organized and are "free" to exploit the advantage of low prices. Low prices encourage overproduction, as producers attempt to make up their losses "on volume," and overproduction inevitably makes for low prices. The land-using economies thus spiral downward as the money economy of the exploiters spirals upward. If economic attrition in the land-using population becomes so severe as to threaten production, then governments can subsidize production without production controls, which necessarily will encourage overproduction, which will lower prices—and so the subsidy to rural producers becomes, in effect, a subsidy to the purchasing corporations. In the land-using economies, production is further cheapened by destroying, with low prices and low standards of quality, the cultural imperatives for good work and land stewardship.

.   .   .

This sort of exploitation, long familiar in the foreign and domestic colonialism of modern nations, has now become "the global economy," which is the property of a few supranational corporations. The economic theory used to justify the global economy in its "free market" version is, again, perfectly groundless and sentimental. The idea is that what is good for the corporations will sooner or later—though not of course immediately—be good for everybody.

That sentimentality is based, in turn, upon a fantasy: the proposition that the great corporations, in "freely" competing with one another for raw materials, labor, and market share, will drive each other indefinitely, not only toward greater "efficiencies" of manufacture, but also toward higher bids for raw materials and labor and lower prices to consumers. As a result, all the world's people will be economically secure—in the future. It would be hard to object to such a proposition if only it were true.

But one knows, in the first place, that "efficiency" in manufacture always means reducing labor costs by replacing workers with cheaper workers or with machines.

In the second place, the "law of competition" does *not* imply that many competitors will compete indefinitely. The law of competition is a simple paradox: Competition destroys competition. The law of competition implies that many competitors, competing on the "free market" without restraint, will ultimately and inevitably reduce the number of competitors to one. The law of competition, in short, is the law of war.

In the third place, the global economy is based upon cheap long-distance transportation, without which it is not possible to move goods from the point of cheapest origin to the point of highest sale. And cheap long-distance transportation is the basis of the idea that regions and nations should abandon any measure of economic self-sufficiency in order to specialize in production for export of the few commodities, or the single commodity, that can be most cheaply produced. Whatever may be said for the "efficiency" of such a system, its result (and, I assume, its purpose) is to destroy local production capacities, local diversity, and local economic independence. It destroys the economic security that it promises to make.

This idea of a global "free market" economy, despite its obvious moral flaws and its dangerous practical weaknesses, is now the ruling orthodoxy of the age. Its propaganda is subscribed to and distributed by most political leaders, editorial writers, and other "opinion makers." The powers that be, while continuing to budget huge sums for "national defense," have apparently abandoned any idea of national or local self-sufficiency, even in food. They also have given up the idea that a national or local government might justly place restraints upon economic activity in order to protect its land and its people.

The global economy is now institutionalized in the World Trade Organization, which was set up, without election anywhere, to rule international trade on behalf of the "free market"—which is to say on behalf of the supranational corporations—and to *over*rule, in secret sessions, any national or regional law that conflicts with the "free market." The corporate program of global "free trade" and the presence of the World Trade Organization have legitimized extreme forms of expert thought. We are told confidently that if Kentucky loses its milk-producing capacity to Wisconsin (and if Wisconsin's is lost to California), that will be a "success story." Experts such as Stephen C. Blank, of the University of California, Davis, have recommended that "developed" countries, such as the United States and the United Kingdom, where food can no longer be produced cheaply enough, should give up agriculture altogether.

The folly at the root of this foolish economy began with the idea that a corporation should be regarded, legally, as "a person." But the limitless destructiveness of this economy comes about precisely because a corporation is *not* a person. A corporation, essentially, is a pile of money to which a number of persons have sold their moral allegiance. Unlike a person, a corporation does not age. It does not arrive, as most persons finally do, at a realization of the shortness and smallness of human lives; it does not come to see the future as the lifetime of the children and grandchildren of anybody in particular. It can experience no personal hope or remorse, no change of heart. It cannot humble itself. It goes about its business as if it were immortal, with the single purpose of becoming a bigger pile of money. The stockholders essentially are usurers, people who "let their money work for them," expecting high pay in return for causing others to work for low pay. The World Trade Organization enlarges the old idea of the corporation-as-person by giving the global corporate economy the status of a super-government with the power to overrule nations.

I don't mean to say, of course, that all corporate executives and stockholders are bad people. I am only saying that all of them are very seriously implicated in a bad economy.

Unsurprisingly, among people who wish to preserve things other than money—for instance, every region's native capacity to produce essential goods—there is a growing perception that the global "free market" economy is inherently an enemy to the natural world, to human health and freedom, to industrial workers, and to farmers and others in the land-use economies; and, furthermore, that it is inherently an enemy to good work and good economic practice.

I believe that this perception is correct and that it can be shown to be correct merely by listing the assumptions implicit in the idea that corporations should be "free" to buy low and sell high in the world at large. These assumptions, so far as I can make them out, are as follows:

1. That there is no conflict between the "free market" and political freedom, and no connection between political democracy and economic democracy.

2. That there can be no conflict between economic advantage and economic justice.

3. That there is no conflict between greed and ecological or bodily health.

4. That there is no conflict between self-interest and public service.

5. That it is all right for a nation's or a region's subsistence to be foreign-based, dependent on long-distance transport, and entirely controlled by corporations.

6. That the loss or destruction of the capacity anywhere to produce necessary goods does not matter and involves no cost.

7. That, therefore, wars over commodities—our recent Gulf War, for example—are legitimate and permanent economic functions.

8. That this sort of sanctioned violence is justified also by the predominance of centralized systems of production, supply, communications, and transportation that are extremely vulnerable not only to acts of war between nations, but also to sabotage and terrorism.

9. That it is all right for poor people in poor countries to work at poor wages to produce goods for export to affluent people in rich countries.

10. That there is no danger and no cost in the proliferation of exotic pests, vermin, weeds, and diseases that accompany international trade, and that increase with the volume of trade.

11. That an economy is a machine, of which people are merely the interchangeable parts. One has no choice but to do the work (if any) that the economy prescribes, and to accept the prescribed wage.

12. That, therefore, vocation is a dead issue. One does not do the work that one chooses to do because one is called to it by Heaven or by one's natural abilities, but does instead the work that is determined and imposed by the economy. Any work is all right as long as one gets paid for it. (This assumption

explains the prevailing "liberal" and "conservative" indifference toward displaced workers, farmers, and small-business
people.)

13. That stable and preserving relationships among people, places,
and things do not matter and are of no worth.

14. That cultures and religions have no legitimate practical or economic concerns.

These assumptions clearly prefigure a condition of total economy. A total economy is one in which everything—"life forms," for
instance, or the "right to pollute"—is "private property" and has a
price and is for sale. In a total economy, significant and sometimes
critical choices that once belonged to individuals or communities
become the property of corporations. A total economy, operating
internationally, necessarily shrinks the powers of state and national
governments, not only because those governments have signed over
significant powers to an international bureaucracy or because political
leaders become the paid hacks of the corporations, but also because
political processes—and especially democratic processes—are too
slow to react to unrestrained economic and technological development on a global scale. And when state and national governments
begin to act in effect as agents of the global economy, selling their
people for low wages and their people's products for low prices, then
the rights and liberties of citizenship must necessarily shrink. A total
economy is an unrestrained taking of profits from the disintegration
of nations, communities, households, landscapes, and ecosystems.
It licenses symbolic or artificial wealth to "grow" by means of the
destruction of the real wealth of all the world.

Among the many costs of the total economy, the loss of the principle
of vocation is probably the most symptomatic and, from a cultural
standpoint, the most critical. It is by the replacement of vocation with
economic determinism that the exterior workings of a total economy
destroy human character and culture also from the inside.

In an essay on the origin of civilization in traditional cultures, Ananda Coomaraswamy wrote that "the principle of justice is the same throughout . . . [It is] that each member of the community should perform the task for which he is fitted by nature." The two ideas, justice and vocation, are inseparable. That is why Coomaraswamy spoke of industrialism as "the mammon of injustice," incompatible with civilization. It is by way of the practice of vocation that sanctity and reverence enter into the human economy. It was thus possible for traditional cultures to conceive that "to work is to pray."

Aware of industrialism's potential for destruction, as well as the considerable political danger of great concentrations of wealth and power in industrial corporations, American leaders developed, and for a while used, certain means of limiting and restraining such concentrations, and of somewhat equitably distributing wealth and property. The means were: laws against trusts and monopolies, the principle of collective bargaining, the concept of 100 percent parity between the land-using and the manufacturing economies, and the progressive income tax. And to protect domestic producers and production capacities, it is possible for governments to impose tariffs on cheap imported goods. These means are justified by the government's obligation to protect the lives, livelihoods, and freedoms of its citizens. There is, then, no necessity that requires our government to sacrifice the livelihoods of our small farmers, small-business people, and workers, along with our domestic economic independence, to the global "free market." But now all of these means are either weakened or in disuse. The global economy is intended as a means of subverting them.

In default of government protections against the total economy of the supranational corporations, people are where they have been many times before: in danger of losing their economic security and their freedom, both at once. But at the same time the means of defending themselves belongs to them in the form of a venerable principle: Powers not exercised by government return to the people. If the government does not propose to protect the lives, the livelihoods, and the freedoms of its people, then the people must think about protecting themselves.

How are they to protect themselves? There seems, really, to be only one way, and that is to develop and put into practice the idea of a local economy—something that growing numbers of people are now doing. For several good reasons, they are beginning with the idea of a local food economy. People are trying to find ways to shorten the distance between producers and consumers, to make the connections between the two more direct, and to make this local economic activity a benefit to the local community. They are trying to learn to use the consumer economies of local towns and cities to preserve the livelihoods of local farm families and farm communities. They want to use the local economy to give consumers an influence over the kind and quality of their food, and to preserve and enhance the local landscapes. They want to give everybody in the local community a direct, long-term interest in the prosperity, health, and beauty of their homeland. This is the only way presently available to make the total economy less total. It was once the only way to make a national or a colonial economy less total, but now the necessity is greater.

I am assuming that there is a valid line of thought leading from the idea of the total economy to the idea of a local economy. I assume that the first thought may be a recognition of one's ignorance and vulnerability as a consumer in the total economy. As such a consumer, one does not know the history of the products one uses. Where, exactly, did they come from? Who produced them? What toxins were used in their production? What were the human and ecological costs of producing and then of disposing of them? One sees that such questions cannot be answered easily, and perhaps not at all. Though one is shopping amid an astonishing variety of products, one is denied certain significant choices. In such a state of economic ignorance it is not possible to choose products that were produced locally or with reasonable kindness toward people and toward nature. Nor is it possible for such consumers to influence production for the better. Consumers who feel a prompting toward land stewardship find that in this economy they can have no stewardly practice. To be a consumer in the total economy, one must agree to be totally ignorant, totally passive, and totally dependent on distant supplies and self-interested suppliers.

And then, perhaps, one begins to *see* from a local point of view. One begins to ask, What is here, what is in my neighborhood, what is in me, that can lead to something better? From a local point of view, one can see that a global "free market" economy is possible only if nations and localities accept or ignore the inherent weakness of a production economy based on exports and a consumer economy based on imports. An export economy is beyond local influence, and so is an import economy. And cheap long-distance transport is possible only if granted cheap fuel, international peace, control of terrorism, prevention of sabotage, and the solvency of the international economy.

Perhaps also one begins to see the difference between a small local business that must share the fate of the local community and a large absentee corporation that is set up to escape the fate of the local community by ruining the local community.

So far as I can see, the idea of a local economy rests upon only two principles: neighborhood and subsistence.

In a viable neighborhood, neighbors ask themselves what they can do or provide for one another, and they find answers that they and their place can afford. This, and nothing else, is the *practice* of neighborhood. This practice must be, in part, charitable, but it must also be economic, and the economic part must be equitable; there is a significant charity in just prices.

Of course, everything needed locally cannot be produced locally. But a viable neighborhood is a community, and a viable community is made up of neighbors who cherish and protect what they have in common. This is the principle of subsistence. A viable community, like a viable farm, protects its own production capacities. It does not import products that it can produce for itself. And it does not export local products until local needs have been met. The economic products of a viable community are understood either as belonging to the community's subsistence or as surplus, and only the surplus is considered to be marketable abroad. A community, if it is to be viable, cannot think of producing solely for export, and it cannot permit importers to use cheaper labor and goods from other places to destroy the local capacity to produce goods that are needed locally. In charity, moreover, it must refuse to import goods that are produced at the cost of human or ecological degradation elsewhere. This principle of subsistence applies not just to localities, but to regions and nations as well.

The principles of neighborhood and subsistence will be disparaged by the globalists as "protectionism"—and that is exactly what it is. It is a protectionism that is just and sound, because it protects local producers and is the best assurance of adequate supplies to local consumers. And the idea that local needs should be met first and only surpluses exported does *not* imply any prejudice against charity toward people in other places or trade with them. The principle of neighborhood at home always implies the principle of charity abroad. And the principle of subsistence is in fact the best guarantee of giveable or marketable surpluses. This kind of protection is not "isolationism."

Albert Schweitzer, who knew well the economic situation in the colonies of Africa, wrote about seventy years ago: "Whenever the timber trade is good, permanent famine reigns in the Ogowe region, because the villagers abandon their farms to fell as many trees as possible." We should notice especially that the goal of production was "as many ... as possible." And Schweitzer made my point exactly: "These people could achieve true wealth if they could develop their agriculture and trade to meet their own needs." Instead they produced timber for export to "the world market," which made them dependent upon imported goods that they bought with money earned from their exports. They gave up their local means of subsistence, and imposed the false standard of a foreign demand ("as many trees as possible") upon their forests. They thus became helplessly dependent on an economy over which they had no control.

Such was the fate of the native people under the African colonialism of Schweitzer's time. Such is, and can only be, the fate of everybody under the global colonialism of our time. Schweitzer's description of the colonial economy of the Ogowe region is in principle not different from the rural economy in Kentucky or Iowa or Wyoming now. A total economy, for all practical purposes, is a total government. The "free trade," which from the standpoint of the corporate economy brings "unprecedented economic growth," from the standpoint of the land and its local populations, and ultimately from the standpoint of the cities, is destruction and slavery. Without prosperous local economies, the people have no power and the land no voice.

(2000)

© Guy Mendes

Author of more than fifty books of fiction, poetry, and essays, WENDELL BERRY has farmed a hillside in his native Henry County, Kentucky, with his wife, Tanya, for more than forty years. He has received numerous awards for his work, including the T. S. Eliot Prize, the Aiken Taylor Award for poetry, the John Hay Award of the Orion Society, the Cleanth Brooks Medal for Excellence in Southern Letters, and the Louis Bromfield Society Award.